GREAT AMERICAN GUIDE TO FINE

WINES

Victor L. Robilio, Jr.

PREMIUM PRESS AMERICA
NASHVILLE, TENNESSEE

GREAT AMERICAN GUIDE TO FINE WINES by Victor L. Robilio, Jr.

Published by PREMIUM PRESS AMERICA

Copyright © 2002 by Victor L. Robilio, Jr.

ISBN 1-887654-32-1

Library of Congress Catalog Card Number 2002091255

PREMIUM PRESS AMERICA gift books are available at special discounts for premiums, sales promotions, fund-raising, or educational use. For details contact the Publisher at P.O. Box 159015, Nashville, TN 37215, or phone toll free (800) 891-7323 or (615)256-8484, or fax (615)256-8624.

Cover and typesetting by: Bob Bubnis/BookSetters
Edited by: Barb Bartels

First Edition 2002
1 2 3 4 5 6 7 8 9 10

TABLE OF CONTENTS

FOREWORD

Victor and Kay have done it again! From their base in Memphis, they bring a whole world of wine and food enjoyment in this, their latest book.

I am especially pleased that they have taken note of wine's role in a delightful quality of life. You can enjoy–and learn from–the pleasures of their travels by tasting the same wines in your own home.

Vic and Kay also remind us of the marvelous *60 Minutes* program in which Morley Safer featured the phenomenon of wine and the heart–where independent medical researchers showed us that, for most people, wine in moderation can have healthy heart outcomes. Since

5

that broadcast, additional research covering a broad variety of medical conditions has focused on the role of wine in the enhancement of our health.

Let me encourage everyone to enjoy Vic's and Kay's recommendations on wines, try the delicious recipes, and then visit **us** in Napa Valley!

Sincerely,

Robert Mondavi

INTRODUCTION

*T*hanks for choosing *A Guide to Fine Wines*. It furnishes you with lots of information packed in a small-size format. In his foreword to this book, Robert Mondavi, the "Dean" of American wine, backs up my family's thoughts about wine appreciation. His kind words about our wine knowledge and experience make this book a very credible choice for your wine library.

I sincerely believe this guide will help you savor and enjoy the most civilized beverage created naturally by God and mankind. It is authentic and unbiased, and stands as a new beginning for wine appreciation.

My wife, Kay, and I have traveled to the most important fine-wine areas and gourmet food districts of this world. One of our favorite pastimes is pairing excellent wines with their delicious food counterparts, which Chapter VI explains. This marrying of flavors is what the "good life" is all about.

Bon Appetit!

CHAPTER I

World Grape Growing at a Glance

I feast on wine and bread, and feasts they are. —Michelangelo (1475-1564)

ITALY

THE ROMANS SPREAD GRAPE GROWING (VITICULTURE) and winemaking (viniculture) wherever their legions of soldiers were deployed. Remnants of their vineyards still dot the countryside of France, Germany, Spain, Israel, Egypt, Hungary, Italy, and

Greece. Visitors to these countries can enjoy seeing some of the remaining caves, cellars, and wineries.

Romans first introduced the world to **Cabernet Sauvignon** (from Bordeaux) and **Gewürztraminer** (from Alsace) grapes. In later centuries, the Italians developed the grapes for **Chianti**, **Gavi**, **Barolo**, **Gattinara**, and **Brunello di Montalcino**. Two outstanding grapes the Italians use today are **Nebbiolo** (Barolo) and **Sangiovese** (Chianti).

Don't be confused. Most Italian wines today are still named after geographical and historical designations. Banfi Vintners, Kobrand Corporation, and A.V. Imports are three American importers that have portfolios of exceptional quality, vintage Italian wines.

Many new excellent vineyards of Cabernet Sauvignon, Chardonnay, and Pinot Grigio varietals have been planted since 1980 in Italy. They are now reaching into the wine cellars of American homes.

ITALIAN WINE SUGGESTIONS:

Cecchi Sangiovese or Chianti Classico
Luna Di Luna Pinot Grigio / Chardonnay blend
Pighin Pinot Grigio
Banfi Brunello di Montalcino
Principessa Gavi

FRANCE

France's **Cabernet Sauvignon** (from the Armenian Mountains) is undoubtedly the best grape for aging fine red wine anywhere, anytime, and by anyone. This grape was planted in Bordeaux, France, by the Phoenicians long before the Gallic Wars of 44 B.C.

The **Pinot Noir** grape (from France) produces softer and subtler red wines. It has some aging qualities but not the 25-year aging ability that the Cabernet Sauvignon retains. Pinot Noirs actually go well with saltwater and freshwater fish. Believe it or not, wine snobs, Pinot Noirs should be chilled to cellar temperature, around 57 to 62 degrees. Michael Mondavi has suggested that we follow this proper serving temperature for red wines. A Bouchard Pere et Fils French Burgundy firm owner has suggested the same lower serving temperature as well.

France also produces **Merlot** grapes. The great Chateau Petrus (St. Peter) from the Pomerol area of France is produced with a preponderance of Merlot grapes. Also, a great Merlot-based St. Emilion wine–Chateau Ausone (named after Ausonius, the Roman poet)–is exquisite, long lasting, and without duplication. Shellfish and any sea crustacean, chicken, and quail go well with the lighter style Merlots. Heavier dishes, such as beef tenderloin, prime beef, or lamb, deserve heavier bodied Merlots. The wine snobs will argue against red wines with fish, but it's perfectly acceptable.

We owe many thanks to the unknown crusader that brought the magnificent deep-bodied, robust, full-flavored **Syrah** grape from Persia (known today as Iran) to the Rhone River Valley of France. This was in the turbulent 12th century. The Rhone River Valley's sun produces such an array of fine wines that use the Syrah grape as their blend base. This grape will, undoubtedly, be an excellent U.S. seller in the next few years.

Chardonnay (from the Champagne and Burgundy regions of France) is the most important white grape in France and is grown for Champagnes and white Burgundies. French Chardonnay is usually crisper, less buttery, less fragrant, and contains more of a light and fleeting lemon-citrus bouquet. Great differences in quality exist when you shop among unknown producers.

Beware of bad vintage French Chardonnay. Usually an American importer like Kobrand Corporation can be your guide to quality. When choosing French Chardonnay, don't count on vintage charts or vintage snobs. Chardonnay wine has been a "hot item" with American wine snobs. They have overtalked and overworked the use of this name at dinner parties. Also, they pick out "easy-to-pronounce" Chardonnay brand names from various parts of the wine world. But it is necessary to try Chardonnays from all areas of the civilized world. The snobs don't experiment, nor do they learn anything by tasting.

Originating in the France-Loire River Valley and Bordeaux areas, French **Sauvignon Blanc**, the key grape in producing great white Bordeaux wines, is also known in France as **Fumé Blanc**. In the United States, the term Sauvignon Blanc is used, unless the wine has a more steely or rocky taste. The French Loire Valley Sauvignon Blanc wines are usually more robust than their Bordeaux-produced Sauvignon Blanc cousins.

> *The first wine tour of Europe that Kay and I took changed our lives. Why? It exposed us to the great wines and chateaus of France.*

Guide to Fine Wines

The first wine tour of Europe that Kay and I took changed our lives. Why? It exposed us to the great wines and chateaus of France. We stayed at Chateau Bouscaut, which in 1973 was owned by an American family, the Dillons. Enclosed is our letter to my family relating our excitement and enthusiasm. Gerald Asher, the British "Master of Wine" and wine editor of *Gourmet Magazine*, planned our itinerary and scheduled our every stop. The trip, which changed our wine and food tasting ability and lifestyle, can never be copied.

Dear Mom, Dad, and John,

We are having a wonderful trip. Archibald Johnston of Nathaniel Johnson and Fils, son of the owner, took us to Chat. Lafite, Mouton, Du Cru Beaucaillou, and Beychevelle, today. We saw Baron Philipe Rothschild's (of Mouton Rothschild) private wine cellar of over 130,000 bottles. It contains only the best French clarets: 1874 Chat. Latour, 1929 Chat. Petrus, 1924 Chat. Palmer, 1929 Chat. Rausan Segla, etc. We tasted 1970 Lafite and 1972 Mouton straight from the aging casks. Tres Bien!

We were served a five course meal by candlelight by a young French girl here a Chat. Bouscaut. The Chateau is very beautiful and has very modern baths and facilities. It is decorated in authentic furniture from the William and Mary period.
Love,
Kay & Vic

France's best producer is Louis Jadot. The late Andre Gagey long ago instituted Jadot's strict quality controls. His son, Henry Pierre Gagey, carries on his tradition of "no compromise" with vintage quality. In 1979, my wife, Kay, and I enjoyed a delightful lunch at a restaurant with Andre. He brought along an old 1955 Corton Pouget in a wicker basket from his home in Beaune. *C'est magnific* for the taste!

The Jean Abeille family operates Mont Redon. I have visited the winery three times–in 1973, 1975, and 2000. My favorite wine from this area is Mont Redon Chateauneuf du Pape. It ages well and is not too heavy bodied or tannic tasting. Place the smooth, rich, full-flavored taste of the Syrah grape in your wine memory banks and retain it. A sun-enriched grape, like the Syrah, is without duplication.

The Loire River Valley produces exquisite **Chenin Blanc**. Also, an excellent sparkling wine is made from this grape, and it is called Bouvet Saphir. It is produced in caves along the banks of the Loire River. Bouvet Saphir is very dry and crisp, with many tiny powerful bubbles. This sparkler is "no sissy." It will hold its own with most food and costs around $13 per bottle. The bubbles explode in your mouth with a full creamy effervescence and leave a steely-rocky aftertaste. Use Chenin Blanc for tailgate parties, picnics, and sandwich-driven lunches. The wine snobs often avoid Chenin Blanc because it is not in their $15 to $20 wine-cost range. You can purchase Chenin Blanc for about $10 to $12.

Alsace sits as a small wine area in northeast France. The area is shaped like a worm and stretches roughly from Strasbourg on the north end to Colmar on the

Julius Caesar's memories of the Gallic wars describe the caves. "I know they are still there because I viewed them, but the French have built their large, fancy homes in front of the caves."

south end. Too many times over many centuries, wars have caused this small area to change hands between France and Germany. Julius Caesar brought the **Gewürztraminer** grape to Alsace during the Gallic wars around 44 B.C. from the Tyrolian Mountains of northern Italy.

The flowery, spicy aroma and bouquet of Gewürztraminer goes well with barbecue or heavier pork dishes–even honey-baked turkey. Wine snobs don't drink Gewürztraminer, but make sure you don't miss out on the exquisite aroma and fresh taste of this wine. It is usually a good buy around $10 to $12 per bottle.

FRENCH WINE SUGGESTIONS:

Louis Jadot Chardonnay
Louis Jadot Macon Blanc
Louis Jadot Gevrey Chambertin
Louis Jadot Beaujolais Villages
Chateau Coufran Bordeaux
Mouiex St. Emilion & Merlot
Dopff Au Moulin Gewürztraminer

GERMANY

The Roman legions planted the first grapevines in Germany at Trier, the Roman (German) capital. Until that time, the Germans drank mead (honey wine), worshipped Thor (the tree god), and didn't produce wine until Julius Caesar arrived there around 44 B.C. Thank you Julius Caesar!

White Riesling, also known as **Johannisberg Riesling**, is the grape most associated with Germany. The good Benedictine monks discovered the Riesling grape at the Abbey of St. John the Baptist, near Bingen on the Rhine River in 1775. Thomas Jefferson, one of our most intelligent and most inventive American presidents, visited Germany in 1788 and loved the country's wines.

Along the Rhine and Moselle Rivers, where many grapes are grown, the banks are steep and sloping. Besides that, Germany has a short grape-growing period of only around 90 days. Because of these constraints, all wine enthusiasts should admire the tenacity and resourcefulness of the German grape growers.

Riesling grapes produce soft wines, lower in alcohol because of their blended fruity and acidic flavors. Germany produces more than just Rieslings though. Today we are seeing a new interest in fine German wines. They are light, delicate, lower in alcohol content than many others, and easy to digest. Most are especially good with fine cheese, crusty bread, and fresh apples.

The fresh **Riesling Kabinetts** of Germany present a good alternative if you don't like dry white wines, such as Sauvignon Blanc or Chardonnay. Most Kabinetts are 2% to 3% in natural residual grape sugar. Truly dry wines have very small traces of residual sugar, usually only .25% to .35%. Spätlese wines are usually 3% to 4% natural residual grape sugar. The term Spätlese simply means "late harvested."

Most of the better quality German wines are left to age for a few years, but the fresh taste of young German wine can't be beat. Buy them young and drink them young. The wine snobs prefer the old German wines that have lost their freshness, but who cares what the snobs preach anyway?

GERMAN WINE SUGGESTIONS:

Cellars International Monchof Astor Kabinett
Deinhard Piesporter Riesling
Cellars International Gunderloch Diva Spätlese

CHILE & ARGENTINA

The South American countries of Chile and Argentina possess very old traditions of growing grapes and making wine-dating to the 16th century. It was only in the late 19th century that European "vitis vinifera" grapevines were brought to South America. Today, world-class wines are made by both countries. In the 19th century, Chilean pioneer Don Francisco Ramon Undurraga imported higher quality European grape varieties. His choices were **Cabernet Sauvignon**, **Riesling**, **Sauvignon Blanc**, and **Pinot Noir**. He also used handmade Yugoslavian oak barrels to age his wines. The Vina Undurraga's estate is located in the famous Maipo Valley of Chile.

Chile's Concha y Toro's Casillero del Diablo Cabernet Sauvignon wine has a legend attached to it. The name in Spanish means "the devil's cave." As the story goes, the disappearance of older aged wine was a problem, so the villagers and wine cellar workers were told a devil lived in this wine storage cave. The legend kept people out of the storage cave and away from the aging Casillero

Cabernet Sauvignon, which needs proper wood aging to add complexity to this excellent wine.

Don't be timid about asking about your favorite wine store to stock the wines of Argentina, which are great buys. Many sell for half the price of similar French and American wines. They are also usually very well made. They sometimes use grafted rootstocks if they wish to increase acreage production.

Both Chile and Argentina have ungrafted European grapevines (no phylloxera). They both use modern winemaking procedures. Many 21st-century modern wineries now exist in Argentina. The infusion of American and European capital has immensely helped quality control.

Nicolas Catena has become the innovative "Robert Mondavi" of Argentina. In 1983 he started his quest for super quality wines from the Mendosa area. He used the research and experimentation that he had witnessed at Robert Mondavi and other great California wineries to start a quality wine revolution in the Mendosa area.

CHILEAN WINE SUGGESTIONS:

Concha y Toro Casillero del Diablo Cabernet Sauvignon
Walnut Crest Sauvignon Blanc

Errazuriz Wild Fermented Chardonnay
Caliterra Cabernet Sauvignon
Cousino Macul Finis Terrae Red
Undurraga Merlot
Luis Felipe Edwards Cabernet Sauvignon Estate

ARGENTINIAN WINE SUGGESTIONS:

Uvas del Sol Cabernet Sauvignon Reserve
Alamos Ridge Malbec
Catena Chardonnay
Etchart Chardonnay
Valentin Bianchi Malbec
Uvas Del Sol Torrontes Blanc

AUSTRALIA

A country geographically about the same size of the United States, Australia has a population of only 8,000,000. The wine areas in the southeast are near Adelaide–similar in location to Florida on a U.S. map.

The first wine grapes were planted in Australia from South Africa in 1788. Then, during the 1840s, waves of European immigrants started to arrive and plant vines in South Australia, Victoria, and New South Wales.

The wine industry in Australia is very similar chronologically to the California wine industry's vineyard development. Both ran like two ships at night, unaware of each other's development or course. Distance was their nemesis. In its 200-year-plus wine history, Australia has had a problem with its distance from most key wine-consuming markets. However, this is not true today. You can ship wine from Australia in air-conditioned or insulated 40-foot containers. And most merchant ships are more dependable and take less time to arrive in the Northern Hemisphere ports than they did in the past.

Australia presently is noted for many high-quality and attractively priced wines. Six large Australian corporations dominate wine production. They are: South Corp., Wines Pty. Ltd., BRL Hardy Ltd., Simeon Wines Ltd., Orlando-Wyndham Group Pty. Ltd., and Berinfer Blass Wine Estates.

Some excellent Australian wines include Jacob's Creek, Tyrrell's, and Stonehaven. Jacob's Creek produces a very good **Chardonnay-Semillon** blend. It is dry with a nice balance of flavors. They also turn out a **Cabernet/Shiraz** blend of excellent quality. It is made softly dry, with a mellow, rich, mature bouquet.

AUSTRALIAN WINE SUGGESTIONS:

Jacob's Creek Merlot
Stonehaven Chardonnay
Tyrrell's Shiraz "McLaren Vale" Reserve
Jacob's Creek Cabernet / Shiraz
Stonehaven Shiraz
Alkoomi Sauvignon Blanc
Simon Gilbert Chardonnay

SHOW THOSE WINE SNOBS
YOUR AUSSIE VOCABULARY

Bail: Depart or leave
Beaut: Beautiful, good
Bender: Heavy drinking session
Berk: Idiot, fool
Billabong: Waterhole or stagnant lake or pool.
Cab Sav: Cabernet Sauvignon wine
Cool bananas: Everything's great, fine!
Crash hot: Wonderful, the best
Feed: Meal
Fess up: Confess, own up
Good day, mate: Hello

Goonie: Cheap cask wine
Mate: Friend
Neato: Excellent
Plonk: Cheap wine
Plonk: Wine addict
Ring-in: An outsider, non-local or regular at a club or pub
Roos: Kangaroos
Squiz: Have a look at
Tucker bag: Food bag in the bush
Tucker chute: Mouth
Zonked: Exhausted

NEW ZEALAND

$\int$outheast of Australia, New Zealand is shaped much like our own Florida Keys, even though it is much larger. New Zealand produces many superb **Sauvignon Blancs**, including Isabel Estate and Goldwater. These wines have a dry and crisp taste, along with superb tangerine-lemon-melon bouquet.

New Zealand is about the size of California. It has both a north and a south island. The largest city, Auckland, is located on the north island, along with many quality wineries adjacent to Hawke's Bay, Martinborough, and Waiheke Island. The New Zealand "jewel" of all wine areas is Marlborough, the "Napa Valley" of New Zealand. Surrounded by tall mountains, the beautiful valley of Marlborough is planted mostly with Sauvignon Blanc grapes. The Marlborough Valley has the Wairau River meandering through its rolling vineyards, discharging its water into Cloudy Bay. Marlborough's climate is similar to the Burgundy area of France. Lots of sunshine gives this valley's grapes a perfect balance of acid-sugar levels.

Today, New Zealand produces some of the world's best Sauvignon Blanc wines. Michael and Robin Tiller own Isabel Estate Vineyard Wines and produce world-class wines. They have become the "Robert Mondavi" of this island nation. New Zealand Sauvignon Blanc is drier and more Sancerre-like in taste than other world vineyards of Sauvignon Blanc.

NEW ZEALAND SUGGESTIONS:

Isabel Estate Vineyard Chardonnay
Isabel Estate Vineyard Pinot Noir
Isabel Estate Vineyard Sauvignon Blanc
Isabel Estate Vineyard Riesling
Goldwater "DogPoint" Marlborough Sauvignon Blanc
Saint Clair Estate Riesling
Piper's Brook 9th Island Sauvignon Blanc

CHAPTER II

A Short History of U.S. Grape Growing

A bottle of wine contains more philosophy than all the books in the world.
—Louis Pasteur

Wine snobs usually attribute the founding of California wines to a famous vintner or politician. Not true! California wines owe their beginnings to Franciscan Padre Junipera Serra.

Padre Serra was sent north from the Baja Peninsula of Mexico to California. His goal was to convert the Indians to Christianity. He was a kindly and compassionate Franciscan Padre but somewhat hindered with a crippled leg. On July 16, 1769, he opened "San Diego de Alcala," the first mission in California.

The fourth mission, San Gabriel Arcangel, was founded on September 8, 1771, by two of Father Serra's associates; Father Pedro Cabon and Father Angel Somera. It was the "Queen of Missions." The first winery built in California was located at this prosperous location. The grape planted and grown by the Franciscans was called the mission grape. It was not of outstanding quality, but produced average-quality wine for the dinner table and food use.

Padre Serra continued his chain of missions northward, as far as Sonoma. The 650-mile road connecting each mission was called "El Camino Real" or, in English, "The King's Highway." Any traveler, weary or sick, could get a glass of wine and some bread or fruit at the hospitable missions.

Padre Serra founded such cities as Santa Barbara and San Francisco. Both were first used as missions to convert the Indians. Sometimes the Spanish soldiers with Padre Serra misbehaved and were eliminated by the Indians. Padre Serra, being very cautious, always dropped mustard seed along his route from Baja, Mexico, to San Francisco. This way, even if he lacked having soldiers as guides, in the spring he could find his way home by following the mustard wildflowers.

Also around 1769, across the country in Virginia, Thomas Jefferson entertained friends at his home in Monticello, introducing them to many wines. He had two rules about what he served. First, you stock in your cellar "just about" any and every wine produced–American and foreign. Second, you taste them all, and serve any and all to your friends.

Snobs wouldn't drink American Muscadine or Scuppernong wine, but Jefferson did. He also served sweet Chateau d' Yquem, semi-sweet Schloss Johannisberger Spatlese, and "bone dry" Chateau Margaux or "bone dry" Hospice de Beaune Chambertin. What a great palate he possessed and what a remarkable ability to deflate the wine snob of his time.

Other locations around the country, including New York State, Missouri, and Ohio, had large wineries and immense vineyards in the early history of our country.

Today many picturesque "family wine farms" exist from across the country, producing good-quality wines at affordable prices. Stop, taste, enjoy, and take home their wines and local food products.

CHAPTER III

Northern California

> *Wine brightens the life and thinking of anyone.*
> —*Thomas Jefferson (1743-1826)*

The **Napa Valley** is the "mother of all great American wine areas." She was the leader, and the rest of California and America have followed her. A few of Napa's first settlers included the Indians, the conquistadors, Father Serra and the Franciscan padres, the Mexicans, and the American pioneer immigrants.

Another interesting group, the Silver Trail Squatters, also settled in Napa Valley. One member of the Squatters was Robert Louis Stevenson, the great Scottish writer. He lived in the Napa Valley with his American wife near an abandoned silver mine that was close to the Silverado Trail. One of the Stevensons' friends was Jacob Schram, the original founder of Schramsberg Vineyards. Schram often entertained the couple with his wines and grand hospitality. Other early wine pioneers of the region included Charles Krug and the Beringer brothers.

The Napa Valley and the surrounding areas of Sonoma, Yolo, Lake, and Mendecino produce wines with unique taste and style. The area's soil, climate, aging, and wine-making techniques have catapulted Northern California wines to the zenith of quality.

The Carneros wine areas near San Pablo Bay create magnificent Pinot Noirs. Try the Carneros Creek winery Pinot Noir with your next gourmet dinner. Another "Carneros product" called Domaine Carneros Brut Sparkling wine is also impeccable, offering tiny bubbles, a full bouquet and flavor, and a softly dry finish. It is produced by Taittinger of France and The Kobrand Corporation of the U.S.

"Oh, Napa, Oh Napa, where do I begin?" Probably with Robert Mondavi, the greatest winemaker, the most innovative wine person of the late 20th and early 21st centuries.

The dawn of wine excellence began around 1965 in the Napa Valley. Andre Tchelistcheff at that time was the winemaker at Beaulieu Vineyard. His Beaulieu Vineyard Georges de Latour Cabernet Sauvignon 1970 was at the top of Napa wine excellence at that period in wine history. That same year, Joe Heitz produced an exquisite Heitz Cellars Martha's Vineyard Cabernet Sauvignon nearby. And the race for quality continued with the production of Robert Mondavi Cabernet Sauvignon Reserve 1970. Napa Valley hasn't looked back since. The players are numerous, and the area's wines are world-class.

The **Dunnigan Hills** area of Yolo County brings us a fine quality wine selection. John Giguiere and his family produce R.H. Phillips and Kempton Clark wines in an area that is similar to South Dakota. Sometimes a strong wind blows through the grapevines and the wheat fields above the winery. Nothing breaks the wind because the area is almost treeless. The winery is situated near the University of California, Davis, allowing the family the personnel to fit their needs. The magnificent, modern stone structure of the R.H. Phillips winery stands as a state-of-the-art facility and blends in between the hills like a Roman theater. Two excellent wines produced at R.H. Phillips are the Toasted Head Chardonnay and Toasted Head Merlot.

The **Sonoma County** area is legendary for wine excellence. Jack London, the great American outdoors writer of the 19th century, known especially as the author of *Call of the Wild*, lived near the present-day site of Kenwood Winery. Jack London State Historical Park, nearby, is named for him, as well as Kenwood "Jack London" Cabernet Sauvignon from the south part of Sonoma County. Another fine wine from that area is Valley of the Moon Chardonnay.

Luther Burbank, the great seed developer, lived in Santa Rosa during the early part of the 20th century. His home and grounds are open for public tours.

Healdsburg, another picturesque Sonoma town, is also steeped in rich wine history. When you drive through town, stop and park your car. Walk around the square to observe the old town and its hundred-year-old oak trees. Also enjoy the great Italian restaurant located on the "main drag."

Two wines that are real "comers on" in quality and depth of flavor are from Rabbit Ridge (premium) and Selby Wines (super premium). Erich Russell, winemaker for Rabbit Ridge, was nicknamed "the Rabbit" as a track star in college. His winery lies in the Russian River Valley. Susan Selby worked for Erich before starting up her own Selby Wines. St. Francis and Chateau Souverain, two other excellent wineries, are located geographically in the middle of Sonoma County. Chateau Souverain features a gourmet restaurant with a panoramic view of its surrounding vineyards.

Near the town of Sonoma sits Buena Vista, a picturesque winery begun by Agoston Haraszthy. This wine pioneer, a Hungarian immigrant, upgraded California wine by importing top-quality French, Italian, and German varietal grapevines in the 1860s.

Sonoma wines have improved greatly in depth of flavor and quality since 1970, the date California surpassed many European wines in world competition.

NORTHERN CALIFORNIA WINE SUGGESTIONS:

World Class:

Beaulieu Georges de Latour Cabernet Sauvignon
Beringer Private Reserve Cabernet Sauvignon
Beringer Private Reserve Chardonnay
Robert Mondavi Cabernet Sauvignon Reserve
Robert Mondavi Chardonnay Reserve
Robert Mondavi Fumé Blanc Reserve
Opus One
Heitz Cellars Cabernet Sauvignon Martha's Vineyard
Schramsberg Blanc de Noir Sparkling

Excellent Buys:

Beringer Knights Valley Estate Cabernet Sauvignon
St. Frances Sonoma Chardonnay
R.H. Phillips Sauvignon Blanc
Rocking Horse Zinfandel
Rabbit Ridge Merlot
Kenwood "Jack London" Pinot Noir
Beaulieu Vineyards Napa Chardonnay
Robert Mondavi Napa Cabernet Sauvignon
Chateau Souverain Sauvignon Blanc
Carneros Creek Fleur de Carneros Pinot Noir

CHAPTER IV

Southern California

*Drink no longer water, but use a little
wine for thy stomach's sake.*
—St. Paul the Apostle (A.D. 67)

MONTEREY COUNTY:

In 1770, Spanish Padres planted grapes at the San Antonio Mission located in Monterey County, California. Ten years later, Padre grapes were planted at Soledad Mission, presently the location of the SmithHook Winery-Hahn Estates. Etienne Thee began the first commercial winery in Monterey County in 1852. But the real quality wine break for this area was around 1960, when Phillip Tonqui produced the first wines under the Chalone label.

That same year, Professor A.J. Winkler, a viticultural expert from the University of California at Davis classified Monterey County as a place to grow world-class grapes and produce superb wines. He compared the area to Burgundy and Bordeaux in France. The cool evenings and morning fog help produce grapes with a strong varietal character and a soft balance between acid and sugar.

In the mid-1970s, Richard Peterson traveled south from the Napa Valley to run the Monterey Vineyard, near Carmel. Peterson was the winemaker at Beaulieu vineyard and a protégé of Andre Tchelistcheff. He developed superb red wines at Monterey and was a "spark" for other commercial wineries to settle and start up production. Today the area produces a plethora of fine wines.

EDNA VALLEY AND ARROYO GRANDE VALLEY:

In early California history, the San Luis Obispo mission was called San Miguel Archangel. Father Serra and his padres began the mission in 1797 and made the first wine in the county there. The facility prospered and remained open until the Mexican government secularized all the missions. San Miguel Archangel produced many barrels of wine–considered the best quality of all the missions.

The Paso Robles region, located northeast of San Luis Obispo, began its first commercial winery in 1888 by cattle rancher Andrew York. Named York Mountain Winery, it is still the oldest continually operated winery in this county.

Edna Valley, which is south of San Luis Obispo, did not begin to produce commercial wines until after 1968. In that year, Jack Foote, the county farm adviser, planted varietal grapes in Edna Valley to test the area. After his great success, the region hasn't looked back.

In 1973 Norman Goss planted grapevines on Orcutt Road, thus founding Chamisal Vineyard. That same year, unaware that Goss was planting vines, Jack Niven planted vines at Paragon Vineyard.

Arroyo Grande Valley, which is south of Edna Valley, produced its first wine near Lake Lopez in 1879. Pioneers Henry and Rosa Ditmas used Muscat and Zinfandel vines imported from France and Spain. However, the vineyards sat empty until 1974. At that time, Bill and Nancy Greenough bought the old Ditmas Ranch and rejuvenated the Ditmas Old Vine Zinfandel Estate of 3 acres and brought it back to premium wine production. The Greenoughs added 5 more acres and now call the property Saucelito Canyon Winery, which produces outstanding Zinfandels.

SANTA BARBARA:

In the 1970s. Brooks and Kate Firestone of Firestone Vineyards were the two wine anchors in the Santa Barbara area. Today there are more than 40 wineries in that area. Firestone's commercial success was a "flag" that brought other wineries to that region. The Santa Barbara area has cool evenings and hence produces wines of outstanding quality, particularly some of the best Rieslings and Merlots grown in the United States.

Andre Tchelistcheff was an early consultant for the Firestones. His methods of winemaking added greatly to the quality of the Santa Barbara area wines. His Russian birth, French winemaking training, and American production of great red wines at Beaulieu Vineyards helped the Firestones and other wineries in this area excel.

TEMECULA:

Also in the 1970s, Eli Callaway pioneered in the Temecula area near Riverside, California. His winery sits directly west over the mountains of the Roosevelt National Forest from the Coast Mission of San Juan Capistrano.

Callaway is only 23 miles from the Pacific Ocean in a low-pressure area that pulls cool ocean breezes through the mountain passes into the vineyards. Karl Werner, former winemaster at Scho.oss Vollrads in the Rheingau district of Germany designed the original Callaway winery in 1974. He also was winemaker for the vintages of 1974 and 1975. Eli Callaway eventually sold his winery and later went into producing Callaway golf clubs (Big Bertha). What a pioneer!

SUGGESTIONS:

Firestone Gewürztraminer
Firestone Johannisberg Riesling
Peachy Canyon Eastside Zinfandel
Babcock Central Coast Chardonnay
Byron Santa Maria Chardonnay
Carmody McKnight Cabernet
Clos La Chance Central Coast Merlot
Coturri Vineyards Zinfandel
Norman Monster Zinfandel

Guide to Fine Wines

Hahn Estates Chardonnay
J. Lohr Seven Oaks Cabernet Sauvignon
J. Lohr Riverstone Estate Chardonnay
Robert Mondavi Coastal Merlot
Robert Mondavi Coastal Sauvignon Blanc

CHAPTER V

Washington State and Oregon

Bronze is the mirror of the form; wine, of the heart. —Aeschylus

Washington state has a damp, cold climate on the coast, but just over the mountains, the climate helps produce a dry, arid fertile inland. This is particularly true near the town of Yakima. The coastal mountains serve as barriers and impede moisture from reaching the center of the state. Yakima has rich, volcanic soil and rolling hills, with the presence of majestic Mount Adams standing just to the east of Yakima. The Yakima Indians still own large sections of land near Mount Adams.

Guide to Fine Wines

Washington State's wine industry started in 1825 with the planting of grapes at Fort Vancouver by the Hudson Bay Company. Early pioneers of Italian, German, and French origin also planted grapes where they settled. By 1910, grapes were being grown in most areas of the state of Washington because of the early settlers' plantings.

By the year 1903 modern water irrigation had reached the eastern part of the state. A dry, sunny, desert-like area was to become a grape grower's paradise because of this new irrigation. The rich volcanic soils of the Yakima and Columbia Valleys were planted with Italian and German wine grape varietals at this time.

The first commercial scale planting of vineyards was in the 1960s. The predecessors to Columbia Winery and Chateau Ste. Michelle were the "spark plugs" that started these modern commercial vineyard plantings. During the 1970s, Californian Andre Tchelistcheff, a legendary winemaker at that time, tutored early efforts and guided modern winemaking procedures in Washington.

American wine snobs basically avoid the fine wines from these two Northern states, even to the point of verbally assaulting them. Hogue and Columbia are two reputable wineries in the region. Try a Columbia Merlot with lamb chops or veal. It is one

In order to truly understand and enjoy the wines from Washington State, you must first fly to Seattle and rent a car. Then, head for the breathtaking Yakima River Valley. You will have a beautiful drive through the coastal mountain chain. Stop and chill some Hogue Chardonnay in an icy mountain stream and have a mountain picnic as we did. Enjoy God's creations by standing on a high spot and perusing the scenic Yakima River Valley. Focus your binoculars on the bountiful blessings of our wonderful democracy.

of the most robust Merlots on the market. Hogue's Johannisberg Riesling goes well with catfish, halibut, or shrimp. It is semi-dry with enough tartness to handle any fish or fowl dish.

In **Oregon,** farmers have grown wine grapes since 1850, although the commercial growing didn't occur until 1959. In that year, Richard Sommer established Hillcrest Vineyards at Rosenburg. In 1966, David Lett planted wine grapes in the small Willamette Valley community of Dundee. Richard Sommer was the "spark" that gave inspiration to many of the early winemakers. Other Oregon wine pioneers include Dick and Nancy Ponzi, Dick Erath, Bill and Susan Sokol Blosser, and Bill and Virginia Fuller.

The major wine varietals produced in Oregon are Pinot Noir, Chardonnay, Riesling, Pinot Grigio, Cabernet Sauvignon, Muller Thurgau (from Germany), Gewürztraminer, Sauvignon Blanc, Merlot, and Zinfandel.

From 1990 to 2000, the number of wineries in Oregon has increased from 71 to 155. The amount of grape wine varietals planted as of 1999 was a total of 9,800 acres.

Oregon is located on the same latitude as France. They both are at 45 degrees. The state's valleys and regions are similar to Washington State's wine areas. Rainfall varies from only 3 inches in the south Willamette Valley to 14 inches in the Rogue Valley.

Wine appellations to look for on your bottle's label are Rogue Valley, Umpqua Valley, Walla Walla Valley, Willamette Valley, and Oregon. The great preponderance of wineries is located in the Willamette Valley.

WASHINGTON WINE SUGGESTIONS:

Hogue Chenin Blanc
Columbia Cabernet Sauvignon
Hogue Chardonnay
Hogue Late Harvest White Riesling
Columbia Merlot

OREGON WINE SUGGESTIONS:

Panther Creek "Shea" Pinot Noir
Red Hawk Grateful Red
Firesteed Pinot Noir
Firesteed Barbera d'Asti

CHAPTER VI

Food and Wine: Pairings of Flavors

The primary purpose of wine is to make food taste better. —Myra Waldo

Wine snobs may profess that only white wines go with fish and chicken, but they are wrong. Don't laugh. You can serve light red wine with fish or chicken. Just serve the red wine at about 62 degrees, not room temperature.

Cooking with wine adds flavor to any food dish. The alcohol leaves the dish and only the flavor remains when you cook it. Hot-flavored foods over-power most wines. Dopff Moulin Gewürztraminer can hold its own with barbecue ribs or a pulled white pork sandwich with hot barbecue sauce. White

Merlot works well with "hot" Szechwan Chinese foods. Cajun or Mexican foods made with hot peppers can overpower any wine, so don't "miss the boat." Experiment with foods and wines to find the right combinations.

The marriage of food, wine, and champagne is what the good life accomplishes. And the good life should be enjoyed with good friends and family having fun together and not taking each other too seriously. Snobs often don't know how to have fun–how to jest or kid one another. Pomposity is their main dinner conversation subject.

Cheeses and wines belong together. Here are some suggestions:

First, try mild cheeses, such as Jarlsberg, Edam, and Muenster. Serve them with apples, crusty French bread, Chateau Souverain Sauvignon Blanc, and Forest Glen Merlot.

To show my fun-loving side, a favorite dinner toast of mine is: "I wish you live with vigor until you are 91 and I am the last friend you see before you bail out of life". Another toast I like with wine and food is one by Winston Churchill: "Life is too short to drink bad wine."

Serve some stronger cheeses: Brie, Camenbert, and strong Wisconsin or New York State aged Cheddar with Beaulieu Vineyard Napa Valley Cabernet Sauvignon, Robert Mondavi Pinot Noir Reserve, and Beringer Zinfandel.

With super strong (stinky) cheeses, such as Stilton, Blue Vein, and Gorgonzola, rely on the wines that can handle their robustness. They are called Portos. Some excellent shippers are Taylor Fladgate, Grahams, and Dow's Portos. Dow's is usually a little less sweet than the others.

For an enjoyable lunch for two, order and split a Caesar salad, fresh soup, and only one entrée. The Caesar salad can be topped with grilled salmon or chicken. Order the anchovies and salad dressing on the side. Enjoy this lunch with Robert Mondavi Private Selection Coastal Sauvignon Blanc. If you are watching your weight, choose a grilled fish or chicken dish with a bottle of R.H. Phillips Chardonnay. Pasta is also a good choice, but go light on the sauce. Marinara sauce is lighter and usually available in most fine Italian restaurants. Beaulieu Vineyard Coastal Cabernet Sauvignon stands as a good accompaniment to pasta.

Always go from dry to sweet when tasting either wine or food. For example, steak is a dry food that has no sugar. Sweet foods, such as sweet potatoes, ice cream, pie, cake, cranberries etc., have varying degrees of sugar.

Concentrate when you taste wine (or food) by using the tip of your tongue. This helps your mind perceive sweetness or dryness. The sides of your tongue up front give you the amount of fruity acidity (lemon, lime, or grapefruit-type taste). When tasting wine, cup or roll your tongue, sides up, center flat, and inhale air through the wine in your tongue's cup. Exhale through your nose so that your olfactory nerve in your nose is used properly. There are more than 300 distinct odors recognizable by your olfactory nerve at the rear of your nose. White wines are usually judged for a particular grape variety's flavor and its fruit acidity balance.

The sides of your tongue in the back and the roof of your mouth perceive the amount of tannin (roughness on the roof of your mouth) in red wine tasting. Tannin in red wine is like tasting a strong cup of hot tea when you have left the bag in to steep too long. You will find strong tannin taste in young, vintage-dated, European or American Cabernet Sauvignon, Syrah, Zinfandel, or Pinot Noir.

All fine red wines get tannin from the skins of the grapes and the oak casks they are aged in by the winemaker. Also, stems are sometimes left in contact with the fermented red wine to give more tannin. Tannin is nature's own natural preservative, along with the alcohol.

Guide to Fine Wines

Tannin dissipates after proper aging and the wine becomes velvety smooth. Age your red wines to match your own tolerance of tannin in wines served with particular dishes. Sediment found in wine is a good sign that the wine was aged properly. A green mold, sometimes found on the top of your unopened cork, is also acceptable. It means the wine has been properly aged in a cool, dark cellar.

ONE OF VICTOR'S AND KAY'S FAVORITE MEALS

COMPLIMENTS OF THREE OAKS GRILL
2285 GERMANTOWN ROAD SOUTH,
GERMANTOWN TN 38138

PAN-ROASTED SALMON WITH GINGER CRUST
2 servings

2	(8-ounce) skinless salmon fillets
½	teaspoon Kosher salt
¼	teaspoon black pepper, regular grind
2	ounces olive oil
½	cup bread crumb mixture with fresh ginger added
	Soy Cream Sauce
	Black sesame seeds
	Cilantro sprigs

Preheat the oven to 350 degrees. Season both sides of salmon fillets with Kosher salt and black pepper. Place skillet over high heat. After skillet is very hot, add the olive oil. Heat oil until almost smoking. Place salmon fillets in skillet top side down. Sear until golden brown, approximately 1 minute: turn fillets and sear the other side. Remove from heat. Lightly press ginger bread crumb mixture onto the salmon fillets until the tops are completely covered. Bake at 350 degrees until cooked medium. Line 2 round dinner plates each with 2 ounces of Soy Cream Sauce; place salmon fillet in center of plate, crusted side up. Garnish with black sesame seeds sprinkled over the sauce and a sprig of fresh cilantro.

Soy Cream Sauce:
  1 quart

1	tablespoon unsalted butter, soft
1	tablespoon fresh ginger, chopped fine
¼	cup white wine (dry)
1	quart heavy cream
½	cup soy sauce

Melt butter in heavy 1-quart saucepan. Add ginger and cook 10 seconds. Add wine and simmer until wine is nearly evaporated. Add cream. Simmer until thickened. Add soy sauce; mix well. Refrigerate until ready to use.

WINE SUGGESTIONS:

Taft Street Chardonnay or Sauvignon Blanc (California)
Louis Jadot Pouilly Fuisse (France)
Louis Jadot Macon Blanc Villages (France)

CHAPTER VII

Shipping and Storage of Wines and Champagnes

> *Wine cheers the sad, revives the old, inspires the young, makes weariness forget his toil.* —Lord Byron.

In 1789 Thomas Jefferson had a wine shipping and storage problem. He would pick up his wines shipped from France, Germany, or Italy and take them to his home, Monticello. He would never know what to expect when the wines arrived in Virginia. No air conditioning was available in the shipping of the wine and sometimes the sailing ships were blown off their course and ended up in warm Cuba or Puerto Rico where the wine cargoes cooked. Monticello also had no air conditioning, so a spoiling nightmare could develop.

Jefferson used his genius, however, to solve his storage problem by building a wine room in the cool cellar at Monticello. His wooden racks were triangular shaped, with a safety lip across the bottom. Each rack held about 2 1/2 cases (30 bottles). To save room, bottles were often reverse stacked against each other.

Today most legitimate wine importers have "reefers," which are air-conditioned ship containers. Each reefer can protect roughly 1,200 cases from heat damage. In your home all you need is a cool cellar or an air-conditioned room to provide good protection for your aging wines. A window air-conditioning unit also helps in that protection.

Wine ages slowly, lasts longer, and tastes better if it is kept at a constant temperature of 54 to 64 degrees. That includes reds, whites, and sparkling wines. Fine red wines usually last many years if stored at a constant temperature. Snobs often serve reds that are too young, which makes them over tannic.

White wines and sparkling wine do not keep fresh for a long period. French Alsatian white wines, however, age very well. They are an exception to the rule. Keep white wines for no longer than three years in your cellar and sparkling wines for no longer than two years. Snobs will argue with those recommendations, but often they have more money than they do wine knowledge.

Both cold and heat extremes damage wine's freshness. Extreme cold weather causes wines to freeze, then expand and blow the bottle corks out. To protect your wine cellar or storage room, consider adding a small electric heater with an automatic thermostat. The heater will click on when the room temperature falls below 50 degrees Fahrenheit.

Thomas Jefferson would have loved to have had our ability to cool down the shipping and storage of fine wines. He incidentally had a dumb waiter (small automated lift) that transported wine from his cool cellar to his dining room table. What a genius! We should always toast him at all wine get-togethers. He is truly the "heart and soul" of the American inventive spirit. Let us never forget the spirit of this young founder of our republic.

CHAPTER VIII

Opening and Serving Wine

*The soft extractive note of an aged cork
being withdrawn has the true sound of
a man opening his heart.*
—Samuel Benwell

Even though a wine cellar or cool room will protect your aging wines, you will want to have a number of bottles closer at hand. Place a 36- to 40-bottle wine rack next to your refrigerator. The bottom level can hold six bottles of champagne or sparkling wine. Stock the top level with about 17 bottles of ready-to-drink red wines (assorted and two of each flavor). Place the white wines on the rack between the red and sparkling wines. About 17 bottles of white wine is sufficient (two of each flavor). Chill white and sparkling wines a day before your guests arrive. Open bottles as needed.

Obtain a champagne fizzer to cap all unused sparkling bottles; this will save you many dollars from spoilage. A captain's knife with a "wide thin worm" is the best wine opener to use. The quality ones are made in Munich, Germany.

Don't remove the cork "too fast" or your clothing will match the color of your wine. Pour all wine into the glasses with a "slight wrist twist" to the right to stop dripping. Always pour a half glass of wine so it can breathe. Then swirl it very gently in the glass to let the oxygen enter the wine. Voila! The bouquet is an explosion of odors from aging, winemaking techniques, and blending.

WINE GLOSSARY AND PRONUNCIATION LIST

(Phonetics are sometimes Americanized.)

Barolo (barr-oh-low)
   A big robust, long-lived, red wine from Piedmont, Italy. The basis is the Nebbiolo grape.

Brunello di Montalcino (brew-nel-lo dah mon-tal-chee-no)
   A very long-lived and exquisite red wine from Tuscany, Italy, made famous by Dr. Ezio Rivella, who was Banfi Vintner's winemaker.

Burgundy (burr-gun-dee)
   Famous wine area in southeast France, known worldwide for excellent red and white wines.

Cabernet Sauvignon (ka-behr-nay so-veen-yohng)
   Famous red wine grape varietal. Its origin is from Bordeaux, France, but it is sometimes attributed with a Phoenician origin.

Champagne (shahm-pain)
   Famous sparkling wine district in northeast France. Julius Caesar fortified this area and built its first underground storage caves.

Chardonnay (shar-doh-nay)
   Exquisite white wine grape varietal. Its origin is both the Burgundy and Champagne districts of France.

Chenin Blanc (shay-nan-blawnk)
   Excellent white wine grape varietal. Its origin is the Loire Valley of France where it goes by the name of Vouvray, first introduced commercially in the U.S.A. by Robert & Peter Mondavi around 1955.

Guide to Fine Wines

Chianti Classico Riserva D.O.C. (key-aunt-tee)
Superb red wine from the Tuscany area of Italy. It is known world-wide as a good wine with most pasta and meat sauce dishes.

Fumé Blanc (foo-may-blawnk)
French name for Sauvignon Blanc white wine grape varietal. First introduced commercially in the U.S.A. by Robert Mondavi around 1966, Fumé Blanc has a crispy, smoky, rocky finish.

Gattinara (got-tee-nah-ra)
Outstanding red wine produced in the Piedmont area of northern Italy. It's very long-lived and needs proper aging.

Gavi (gah-vee)
A crispy, dry excellent white wine from the Piedmont area of northern Italy, Gavi is named after a German princess. It is superb with fish or chicken dishes.

Gewürztraminer (guh-verts-tra-mee-ner)
This wine is an excellent Alsatian white wine grape varietal with aromatic aroma and bouquet and a totally dry finish. Great with barbecue!

Merlot (mair-lo)
Red wine grape varietal with origins in the St. Emilion and Pomerol parishes of Bordeaux. This noble grape produces a medium-bodied or lighter style red wine.

Nebbiolo (neb-bee-o-low)
Famous red wine grape varietal from Italy. It is said to be the "anchor" for the great Italian red wines.

Pinot Grigio (pee-no-gree-geo)
Noted Italian white wine grape varietal, it produces a very light and delicate white wine. Try the new Danzante by Robert Mondavi and Marchesi de Frescobaldi.

Pinot Noir (pee-no n'war)
Very famous red wine grape varietal, it produces the great red Burgundy wines of France.

Riesling (rees'ling)
Famous German white wine grape varietal that produces low-alcohol, fresh and fragrant German Moselle and Rhine wines. The grape was discovered by Benedictine monks in 1775.

Sangiovese (san-geo-vay-zee)
Excellent Italian red wine grape varietal. It is the basic grape, along with others, for Italian Chianti. In California, it produces a softly dry, excellent red varietal wine.

Sauvignon Blanc (so-vee-yohng-blawnk)
A French white wine grape varietal, it is found both in the Bordeaux and Loire Valley wine areas of France. Its attributes include a light, dry, crisp taste.

Semillon (say-mee-yohng)
Another fine French white wine grape varietal, its origin is Bordeaux, France. Both France and California blend it to make superb dry or sweet wines.

Spatlese (shpate-lay-zuh)

German wine term that means the grapes are late harvested. The sugar content in the grape is higher than in a normal harvest and produces a sweeter wine.

Syrah (see-ra)

A very famous Rhone Valley of France red wine grape varietal, used in both Chateauneuf du Pape and Hermitage–both superb-quality Rhone wines.

Zinfandel (zin-fan-dell)

Excellent California red wine grape varietal with its origin in Apulia, Italy, which is geographically the "heel of the boot" of Italy. Zinfandel is a clone of the Sangiovese grape.

DIRECTORY OF WINERIES

(Note: These wineries are sorted by state, but follow no particular order. They have been sequenced to make the best use of the space allowed.)

ALABAMA

Perdido Vineyards

22100 County Road 47, Exit 45 I-65, Perdido, Alabama, 36562 (334)937-Wine, (334)937-4996~Fax, www.perdidovineyards.com

Wines: Rose Con Rouge, Mardi Gras, Ecor Rouge, Delta Bouquet, Magnolia, White Muscadine, Sweet Muscadine, Demopolis Ecor Blanc, Elberta May Wine, Wine Cooler.

Tastings and tours available daily from 10am-5pm.

"Perdido Vineyards wines are produced from Muscadine grapes. We have a 50 acre Muscadine grape vineyard. (7 times more anti-oxidants)."

ARIZONA

Fort Bowie Vineyards and Orchard Products

156 North Jefferson, Bowie, Arizona, 85605 (520)847-2593, (520)847-2593~Fax

Wines: Table Wine, Champagne, Sparkling Wine, Merlot, Sweetwater, Bowie, Pecan Delight.

Tastings/tours available Monday-Saturday from 8:30am-4pm. Sunday's from 10am-3pm.

Domaines Ellam, Inc.

471 Elgin Road, Elgin, Arizona, 85611 (520)455-4734, (520)455-9309~Fax, www.earl-of-ellam.com

Wines: Table Wine, Champagne, Sparkling Wine, Syrah, Sauvignon Blanc, Cabernet Sauvignon.

Tastings/tours available daily from 10am-5pm.

Guide to Fine Wines

The Village of Elgin Winery
Elgin Complex, Upper Elgin Road, Elgin, Arizona, 85611 (520)455-9039,
(520)455-9039~Fax, www.concentric.net/Elgnwine

Wines: Table Wine, Champagne, Sparkling Wine, Cabernet Sauvignon, Sangiovese,
Sauvignon Blanc, The Village of Elgin, Tombstone Red, The Village of Tubac, St. Vincent,
Chateau Noir, Village of Elgin Cellars.

Tastings/tours available daily from 10am-5pm.

Arizona Vineyards
1830 Patagonia Highway, Nogales, Arizona, 85621   (520)287-7972,
(520)287-2195~Fax

Wines: Table Wines.

Tastings/Tours available daily from 10am-5pm

Dos Cabezas Wineworks
19 B South Windward Way Road, Kansas Settlement, Arizona (520)455-5285, (520)455-
5285~Fax

Wines: Table Wines, Chardonnay, Sangiovese, Pinot Gris.

San Dominique
Post Office Box 8848, Scottsdale, Arizona, 85252   (480)949-8660

Wines: Table Wines, San Dominique.

Tastings/tours available daily from 10am-5pm. Call for physical address.

Kokopellin Winery
2401 West Southern Avenue #374, Temple, Arizona, 85282, (877)A-WINERY, (877)FAX-
KOKO~Fax

Wines: Table Wine, Champagne, Cabernet Sauvignon, Pinot Noir, Zinfandel, Kokopelli,
Paradise Valley, Imperial Kir, Royal Kir.

Tastings available Saturday's and Sunday's from 12pm-5pm, tours by appointment.

Sonoita Vineyard, LTD.

6550 North First Avenue, Tucson, Arizona, 85718, (520)455-5893

Wines: Table Wine, Champagne, Sparkling Wine, Colombard, Cabernet Sauvignon, Merlot.

Tastings/tours available daily from 10am-4pm.

Dark Mountain Winery

13605 East Benson Highway, Vail, Arizona, 85641, (520)762-5777, (520)762-5898~Fax, www.darkmountainbrewery.com

Wines: Table Wine, Champagne/Sparkling Wine, Beer, Riesling, Colombard, Petite Sirah.

Tastings/tours available Monday through Saturday from 10am-6pm, Sunday's from 12pm-6pm.

ARKANSAS

Mount Bethel Winery

5014 Mount Bethel Drive, Altus, Arkansas, 72821, (501)468-2444, www.mtbethel.com

Wines: Table, dessert and fruit wines.

Tastings and tours on request upon arrival.

"Hand-picked grapes, fermented in redwood, aged in wooden barrels. Bottled in the original wine cellar built in the late 1800's. "

Post Familie Winery

1700 St. Mary's Mountain Road, Altus, Arkansas, 72821   (501)468-2741 (501)468-2740~Fax, www.postfamilie.com

Wines: Red, White and Blush Varietals. Ports and Sherries, Sparkling Wines (Champagne method), Grape Juices.

Tastings/tours available Monday-Saturday from 8am-6pm. Tastings only on Sunday's from 12pm-5pm. Picnic gourmet foods available.

"Extensive tasting offering cheese and crackers, informative wine making tour, upscale gift shop offering grape-themed items and wine accessories."

Wiederkehr Wine Cellars, Inc.
Wiederkehr Village, 3324 Swiss Family Drive, Altus, Arkansas, 72821,
(501)468-2611, (501)468-WINE, (501)468-4791~Fax

Wines: Table Wine, Fruit and Berry Wine, Champagne and other Sparkling Wines.

Tastings/tours available daily from 8:30am-4:30pm.

Cowie Wine Cellars, Inc.
101 North Carbon City Road, Paris, Arkansas, 72855   (501)963-3990,

www.cowiewinecellars.com

Wines: Dry, Semi Sweet, Sweet, Fruit and Special Wines.

Tours of Winery and Museum (Arkansas Historic Wine Museum), call for hours.

Snack trays of cheese, crackers, and meats available.

"Wine tours and tasting, bed and breakfast, museum all on site, family owned, award winning wines, small and friendly, great place to visit."

COLORADO

Augustina's Winery
4715 North Broadway, B-3, Boulder, Colorado, 80304   (303)545-2047

Wines: Harvest Gold, WineChick White, WineChick Blues, Ruby, WineChick Rose', Winechick Red, Joi de Vino Chardonnay.

Tastings/Tours available. Call for hours.

"Dedicated to making wine that goes with backpacking adventure, parties, mystery novels, and Cary Grant movies. One-Woman winery!"

Plum Creek Cellars, Ltd.
3708 G Road, Denver, Colorado, 80209   (303)399-7586, (303)399-8037~Fax

Wines: Table wine, Merlot, Cabernet Franc, Cabernet Sauvignon.

Tastings/tours available daily from 9:30-6pm.

Baharav Vineyards
2370 Road 112, Carbondale, Colorado, 81623   (800)ECO-WINE, (970)963-3438~Fax, www.wineplus.com

Wines: Viognier, Chardonnay, Muscat (Muscat Blanc, and Orange Muscat), Dry, Merlot, Cab. Franc, Merlot, Syrah.

Tastings/Tours available by appointment only.

"Ecologically sensitive grape growing. We use our own grapes in wine making. Only organic grape grower/producer in Colorado."

Stoney Mesa Winery Ltd.
1619 2125 Drive, Cedaredge, Colorado, 81413   (970)856-WINE,(970)856-7997~Fax, www.stoneymesa.com

Wines: Cabernet, Sauvignon, Franc, Merlow, Reisling, Gewürztraminer, Chardonnay, Sauvignon Blanc.

Tasting and tours available seven days per week from 11am-5pm.

"Visit one of the highest vineyards in the world in the picturesque Colorado mountains and taste 100% Colorado grown wines."

Pikes Peak Vineyards, Ltd.
3901 Janitell Road, Colorado Springs, Colorado, 80906   (719)576-0075

Wines: Table wine.

Tastings/tours available daily from 12pm-5pm. Restaurant on premises.

Shadow Mountain Cellars, Ltd.
1708 East Lincoln Avenue #1, Fort Collins, Colorado, 80524   (970)493-7345, (970)493-7345~Fax

Wines: Table wine, Chardonnay, Merlot, Sauvignon Blanc.

Tastings/tours available by appointment.

S. Rhodes Vineyards

1368 3700 Road, Hotchkiss, Colorado, 81419   (970)527-5185,(970)527-5185~Fax

Wines: Table Wine, Merlot, Cabernet Franc, Cabernet Sauvignon.

Tastings/tours available by appointment.

Trail Ridge Winery

4113 West Eisenhower Boulevard, Loveland, Colorado, 80537 (970)635-0949,
www.trailridgewinery.com

Wines: Riesling, Gewürztraminer, Chardonnay, Lemberger, Merlot, Cabernet Franc.

Tastings are available during the summer and fall from 11am-5pm daily. Spring hours
are from 11am-5pm Wednesday through Sunday.

"Fine examples of Colorado wine. Located one hour north of Denver and 45 minutes
from Rocky Mountain National Park."

Rocky Hill Winery

18380 Highway 550, Montrose, Colorado, 81401   (970)249-3765,
(970)249-5652~Fax

Wines: Merlot, Gewürztraminer, Chenin Blanc, Cabernet Sauvignon, Riesling.

Tastings/tours available, call first. Picnic area.

"Enjoy great tasting wines by a stream in the shadows of the snow capped Rocky
Mountains."

Cottonwood Cellars

5482 Highway 348, Olathe, Colorado, 81425   (970)323-6224,(970)323-6182~Fax,
www.cottonwoodcellars.com

Wines: Cabernet Sauvignon, Merlot, Chardonnay, Johannisberg Riesling,
Gewürztraminer, Lemberger, Rose of Cabernet.

Tastings and tours available Wednesday-Saturday from 11am-6pm, or by appointment.

"World class full bodied wines from a European style family winery in a lovely country
setting with spectacular mountain vistas."

Canyon Wind Cellars

3907 North River Road, Palisade, Colorado, 81526 (970)464-0888,
(970)464-7920~Fax, www.coloradowine.com

Wines: Chardonnay, Merlot, and Cabernet Sauvignon.

Tastings and Tours available Monday through Saturday from 10am-5pm.

"Taste what world class wine making does for the wonderful grapes of western
Colorado."

Carlson Vineyards, Inc.

461 35 Road, Palisade, Colorado, 81526 (970)464-5554, (970)464-5542~Fax

Wines: Table Wine, Fruit Wine.

Tastings/tours available daily from 11am-6pm.

Debeque Canyon Winery

3941 U.S. Highway 6 & 24, Palisade, Colorado, 81526 (970)464-0550,
loncedar@gj.net

Wines: Syrah, Viognier, Merlot, Cabernet Sauvignon, Claret, Chardonnay, Pinot Noir.

Tastings available. Call for information.

"All wine from Colorado fruit. Beautiful views from the tasting room."

Grande River Vineyards

787 Elberta Avenue, Palisade, Colorado, 81526 (970)464-5867,

(800)COGROWN, (970)464-5427~Fax, www.granderiverwines.com

Wines: Chardonnay, Merlot, Meritage Red, Meritage White, Sauvignon Blanc, Semi
Sweet, Late Harvest Semillon, Port, Blush, Viognier, Syrah.

Tastings/tours available from 9am-5pm during winter/fall seasons, 9am-6pm in the
spring, 9am-7pm during summer. Picnic area and outdoor concerts.

"Colorado's premium wine growing estate, and Colorado's largest grape producer.
Winner of over 200 awards. Eight varieties and twelve wines!"

Plum Creek Cellars

3708 G Road, Palisade, Colorado, 81526   (970)464-7586, (970)464-0457~Fax

Wines: Chardonnay, Merlot, Cabernet Sauvignon, Sangiovese, Cabernet Franc, Pinot Noir, Riesling, Riesling Ice Wine and Palisade Rose.

Tastings/tours available. Call for hours.

"Award winning wines. Tasting room featuring antiques and fine art. Landscaped grounds and covered patio for picnics. Colorado grapes only!"

Rocky Mountain Meadery

3701 G Road, Palisade, Colorado, 81526   (970)464-7899, (970)464-0175~Fax, www.wic.net/meadery

Wines: Award winning Honey wines, Fruit, Port Style Velvets, Carbonated hard Apple and Pear cider.

Tastings available daily from 10am-5pm. Tours by appointment.

"Colorado's only Meadery. Beautiful gift shop and outdoor gazebo with great views of the Book Cliffs and Grand Mesa."

St. Kathryn Cellar Winery, Event Center and Gift Shop, Inc.

785 Elberta Avenue, Palisade, Colorado, 81526   (970)464-9288, (970)464-9124~Fax, www.st-kathryn-cellar.com

Wines: Merlot, Merlot Reserve, Merlot Port, Chard, Chard Reserve, White Merlot, Cameo Rose, Ruby Red, Apple Blossom, Golden Pear, Cranberry Kiss, Blueberry Bliss.

Tastings/tours available daily during the summer from 10am-6pm. Winter hours are from 10am-5pm. Event center seats 200 and attached catering kitchen.

"Friendliest winery. Tasting room and gift shop. Artists have special area for 'local treasures'. Our wines are quality and fun!"

The Vineland Corporation

3533 E Road, Palisade, Colorado, 81526   (970)464-7921, (970)464-0574~Fax

Wines: Chardonnay, Riesling, Merlot, Table Wine, Fruit and Berry Wines.
Champagne/Sparkling Wine, Kosher Wines.

Tastings/tours available Monday-Saturday from 12pm-4pm.

Terror Creek Winery

1750 4175 Drive, Paonia, Colorado, 81428   (970)527-3484, (970)527-3484~Fax

Wines: Table Wine, Chardonnay, Gewürztraminer, Pinot Noir.

Tastings/tours available Memorial Day-Labor Day on Friday's, Saturday's, and Sunday's
from 11am-5pm.

Mountain Spirit Winery, Ltd.

15750 Country Road 220, Salida, Colorado, 81201 (719)539-1175,(719)539-4920~Fax,
www.mountainspiritwinery.com

Wines: Merlot, Chardonnay, Blackberry/Cabernet Franc, Merlot/Rasberry,
Blackberry/Chardonnay.

Tastings/tours available. Winery open on Monday, Thursday, Friday, and Saturday from
11am-5pm. Downtown gallery/tasting room open Monday-Saturday from 10am-5pm.

"We produce award-winning premium wines, many of which are available no-where
else in the world. Beautiful mountain setting."

Steamboat Springs Cellars

2464 Down Hill Drive #8, Steamboat Springs, Colorado, 80487   (970)879-7501,
(970)879-7501~Fax.

Wines: Merlot, Chardonnay, Rabbit Ears Red, Fish Creek Full.

Tastings/tours by appointment.

"Our grapes are 100% Colorado grown. Wine is made in Steamboat Springs. Stop by
and taste wine out of the barrel."

FLORIDA

Dakotah Winery

14365 North Highway 19, Chiefland, Florida, 32626   (352)493-9309,
(352)493-9309~Fax, max@svic.net

Wines: Sweet and Dry

Tastings and tours daily from 10am-5pm, Sunday 12pm-5pm.

"Audubon Bird Sanctuary, wood duck hatchery, miniature sheep."

Lakeridge Winery and Vineyards

19239 U.S. 27 North, Clermont, Florida, 34711   (352)394-8627, (352)394-7490~Fax,
www.lakeridgewinery.com

Wines: Table, Sparkling, and Dessert Wines.

Tastings/tours available seven days per week. Monday-Saturday from 10a.m-5p.m.,
Sunday 11a.m.-5p.m.

"Lakeridge offers extensive assortment of award-winning Florida wines, gourmet foods,
gifts, accessories, picnic grounds and holds monthly themed festivals."

Three Oaks Winery

3348 Highway 79, Vernon, Florida, 32462   (850)535-9463, (850)535-6951~Fax,
www.fl-ag.com

Wines: Conquistador, Carlos, Merlot.

Tastings/tours available from 10am-5pm Wednesday through Saturday. Closed during
the month of January.

"Certified Florida farm winery. Great wines and gift shop."

Chatauqua Vineyards

364 Hugh Adams Road, DeFuniak Springs, Florida, 32435 (850)892-5887
(850)892-9539~Fax

Wines: Chardonnay, Merlot, Carlos, Noble, Blush, Wildflower Honey Muscadine, Port,
Blueberry.

Complimentary tastings/tours available. Call for hours.

"Featuring wines made from muscadine grapes grown in our vineyards, unique to the
Southeast. Also Vinifera and Fruit Wines."

San Sebastian Winery

157 King Street, St. Augustine, Florida, 32084 (888)352-9463, (904)826-1594, (904)826-1595~Fax, www.sansebastianwinery.com

Wines: Port, Cream, Sherry, Sparkling Wine, Dry Varieties, Dry Red, Muscadine.

Tastings/tours available Monday-Saturday from 10am-6pm and Sunday's from 11am-6pm. Final tour daily starts at 4:45pm.

"We offer complimentary guided tours and tastings seven days a week. Gift/gourmet shop on premises. Ample free parking."

GEORGIA

Three Sisters Vineyards, INC.

240 Vineyard Way, Dahlonega, Georgia, 30533 (706)865-0359, (706)865-1531~Fax, www.threesistersvineyards.com

Wines: Cabernet Franc, Merlot, Chardonnay.

Call for information on tastings/tours.

Chateau Elan, LTD.

Highway 211 @ I-85, Braselton, Georgia, 30517 (800)233-9463, (770)307-0836~Fax, www.chateauelan.com

Wines: Table Wine, Flabored Wine, Chardonnay, Cabernet Sauvignon, Merlot, Chateau Elan, Essence de Cabernet, Summer Wine, Autumn Blush, Spring Blossom, Winter Spice.

Tastings/tours available daily from 10am-9pm.

Chestnut Mountain Winery, INC.

Highway 124, Hoschton, Georgia, 30517 (770)867-6914, (770)867-6914~Fax.

Wines: Table Wines, Chardonnay, Cabernet Sauvignon, Merlot, Chestnut Mountain, Phoenix.

Tastings/tours available Tuesday-Saturday from 11am-6pm, Sunday's from 12:30pm-6pm.

Guide to Fine Wines

Habersham Winery
7025 S. Main Street, P.O. Box 808, Helen, Georgia, 30545 (706)878-9463, (706)878-8466~Fax, www.habershamwinery.com

Wines: Creekstone, Habersham Estates, Southern Harvest.

Tastings daily, self guided tours available.

"We produce an extensive variety of wines, ranging from Cabernet to French American Varieties. Many are medal winners!"

Fox Vineyards
225 Highway 11 South, Social Circle, Georgia, 30025 (770)787-5402, (770)787-5402~Fax, www.georgiawineries.com

Wines: Sweet, Dry, Cabernet, Chardonnay, Riesling.

Tastings/tours available from Wednesday through Saturday from 10am-6pm.

Sunday's from 1pm-6pm. Crackers available.

"We offer great customer service, a nice gift shop; lots of things to choose from, as well as excellent wines."

Georgia Wines, INC.
Battlefield Parkway, Ringgold, Georgia, 30707 (706)937-2177, www.georgiawines.com

Wines: Table Wine, Champagne, Fruit and Berry Wine, Muscadine, Concord, Catawba.

Tastings/tours available Monday through Saturday from 11am-6pm.

Wolf Mountain Vineyards
180 Wolf Mountain Trail, Dahlonega, GA 30533 (706) 867-9862 ~(770) 992-9194 www.wolfmountainvineyards.com

Wines: Cabernet Sauvignon, Merlot, Rhone Style Red Blend, and White Blend

Tastings/tours: By appointment before fall 2002; after 12-5 pm Saturday and Sunday or by appointment

Spectacular views from mountaintop vineyards; Hand crafted, limited production wines; hospitality facilities to accommodate weddings, gourmet dinner, corporate retreats.

KANSAS

Holy-Field Vineyard and Winery

18807 158th Street, Basehor, Kansas, 66007   (913)727-9463,
www.winesacrossamerica.com

Wines: Chardonel, Seyval, Melody, Vignoles, Tailgate White, Kaw River Rhine, Sunset Blush, St. Vincent, Chambourcin, Cynthiana, Racy Red, Tailgate Red, Over the Rainbow Raspberry, St. Francis Dessert Wine.

Tastings available daily Monday-Friday from 11am-6pm, Saturday's from 9:30am-6pm, and Sunday's from 12pm-6pm. Tours by appointment. Reservations needed for bus tours, fee of $1.00 per person bus tours only. Wine deck overlooking vineyard available. Bring your own picnic.

"Enjoy international award winning wines and delight in the unique gift shop. We are only minutes from downtown Kansas City."

Davenport Orchards and Vineyards

1394 East 1900 Road, Eudora, Kansas, 66025   (785)542-2278

Wines: Table Wine, Fruit, Berry, Foch, Seyval Blanc, Chardonnel, Davenport.

Tastings/tours available Monday, Wednesday, and Friday's from 4pm-7pm, and Saturday's/Sunday's from 1pm-5pm.

Fields of Flair Winery

Exit 333, Interstate 70, Paxico, Kansas, 66526   (785)636-5560, (785)636-5365~Fax,
www.fieldsoffairwinery.com

Wines: Kansas Chablis, Kansas Cabernet, Golden Harvest, Flinthills Red, Prairie Dew, Vintage One, Golden Delicious, Sweet William, Concord, Cherry Jubilee, Blackberry Jamboree.

Tastings/tours available by appointment.

"First licensed winery in Kansas. Open daily, free wine tasting and tours, located at exit 333, Interstate 70, Paxico, Kansas"

Guide to Fine Wines

Heimhof Winery
26168 Tongonaxie Road, Leavenworth, Kansas, 66048   (913)351-3467

Wines: Riesling, Cabernet, Sauvignon.

Tastings/tours available Monday-Sunday from 12pm-5pm.

Wyldewood Cellars
951 East 119th Street, Peck, Kansas, 67120   (316)554-9462, (316)554-9191~Fax, www.wyldewoodcellars.com

Wines: Elderberry, Blackberry, Cherry, Elderslower, Sand Plum.

Tastings/tours available, call for hours. Banquet facilities and catering.

"International award winning, premium wines, jellies, and syrups, produced from native fruit that tastes as good as Grandma's.

Smoky Hill Vineyards and Winery
212 West Golf Link Road, Salina, Kansas, 67401 (785)825-2515

Wines: Table Wine, Champagne, Sparkling Wine, Fruit and Berry Wine, Seyval, Vignoles, Norton.

Tastings/tours available Monday through Saturday from 10am-8pm, Sunday's from 1pm-5pm.

Twin Rivers Vineyard
5930 West 85th Street North, Valley Center, Kansas, 67147 (316)755-1403

Wines: Table Wines, Seval Blanc, Vidal Blanc.

Call for tasting/tour information.

KENTUCKY

KENTUCKY

Barker's Blackberry Hill Winery
16629 Mount Zion Verona Road, Crittenden, Kentucky, 41030, (859)428-0377,
www.keyagr.com/blackberryhill.htm

Wines: Meade, Blackberry Sweet and Semi Sweet, Cherry Sweet and Semi Sweet.

Tastings available, tours on request. Call for hours. Blackberries available for picking
in July and August. Kool-ade for the kids.

"Come see our winery for wonderful hospitality, great wines, and good people. Unique
recipes available including wine cake!"

Bravard Vineyards and Winery
15000 Overton Road, Hopkinsville, Kentucky, 42240 (270)269-2583

Wines: Table Wines, Foch, Fruit Hill, Countryside, Lady Genevive, Red September,
Penny Royal.

Tastings/tours available Saturday's from 10am-5pm. Other times by appointment.

Broad Run Vineyards
10601 Broad Run Road, Louisville, Kentucky, 40299 (502)231-0372

Wines: Cabernet, Chardonnay, Riesling, Gewürztraminer, Pinot Noir, Sauvignon Blanc,
Syrah, Foch, Chambourcin, Sparkling Wines, and more.

Tasting and tours are available, call first for schedule. Kentucky crafts gift shop on
premises.

"Experience premium estate-bottled wines from the pastoral beauty of the 25 acres of
vineyards, to the hospitality of the tasting room."

Guide to Fine Wines

LOUISIANA

Pontchartrain Vineyards

81250 Highway 1082, Bush, Louisiana, 70431   (985)892-9742,
(985)892-9742~Fax, www.pontchartrainvineyards.com

Wines: Fine Louisiana table wines in the classic French tradition.

Tastings available Wednesday through Friday from 10am-5pm, Saturday from 10am-4pm, and Sunday from 12pm-4pm. Tours available for groups by appointment. Fee of $3.00 per person for tasting. Bring a picnic and sit on the terrace.

"Our French provincial tasting room overlooks hillside vineyards. Our wines are distinctive: made to compliment Louisiana cuisine. Located just north of New Orleans."

Casa De Sue Winery

14316 Hatcher Road, Clinton, Louisiana, 70722   (225)683-5937,
(225)683-6623~Fax

Wines: Blueberry Dry, La Rosa Dry, Carlos Dry, Nobel, Embrace, Allons Danse, La Louisiane, Blueberry Sweet, La Rosa Sweet, Jambalaya, Blueberry Dessert.

Tastings and tours available Monday-Saturday from 10am-6pm, closed Sunday.

"First licensed winery in Louisiana. See beautiful vineyard next to winery."

Amato's Winery

12415 West Black Cat Road, Independence, Louisiana, 70443 (504)878-6566,
(504)878-6566~Fax

Wines: Fruit, Strawberry, Blueberry, Orange, Muscadine.

Tastings/tours available soon, call for information. Restaurant opening soon.

"Unique fruit wines. Fruit grown in the South. Town home of the Orange Festival of Belle Chase, Ponchatoula Strawberry Festival.

Feliciana Cellars Winery
1848 Charter Street, Highway 10, Jackson, Louisiana, 70748   (225)634-7982, (225)634-3254~Fax, www.felicianawinery.com

Wines: French Hybrid (Blanc Da Bois), Muscadine Wines-Dry to Sweet.

Tastings/tours available Monday-Friday 10am-5pm, Saturdays from 9am-5pm, Sundays 1pm-5pm. Closed New Years, Easter, Thanksgiving, Christmas.

"Largest winery in Louisiana-Gift shop with unique items for the wine lover."

MARYLAND

Catoctin Vineyards
805 Greenbridge Road, Brookeville, Maryland, 20833   (301)774-2310, (301)774-2310~Fax

Wines: Chardonnay, Chardonnay Oak Fermented, Johannisberg, Riesling, Cabernet Sauvignon, Merlot, Chambourcin, Eye of the Orioce, Eye of the Beholder, Mariage.

Tastings/tours available, call for times. $3.00 for souvenir glass.

"Taste fine wines and tour winery in a peaceful country atmosphere for a thrill of a lifetime."

Boordy Vineyards
12820 Long Green Pike, Hydes, Maryland, 21082   (410)592-5015, (410)592-5385~Fax

Wines: Table Wines, Champagne, Grape Juice, Seyval Blanc, Chardonnay, Cabernet Sauvignon.

Tastings/tours available Monday-Saturday from 10am-5pm, Sunday's 1pm-5pm.

Cygnus Wine Cellars
3130 Long Lane, Manchester, Maryland, 21102   (410)374-6395

Wines: Table Wines, Champagne, Sparkling Wine, Vidal Blanc, Chancellor, Cabernet Sauvignon, Cygnus, Royele.

Tastings/tours available Saturday's and Sunday's from 12pm-5pm.

Elk Run Vineyards

15113 Liberty Road, Mt. Airy, Maryland, 21771   (410)775-2513,(410)875-2009~Fax, www.elkrun.com

Wines: Cabernet Sauvignon, Pinot Noir, Chardonnay, Gewürtz Traminev.

Tastings/tours available Tuesday-Saturday from 10am-5pm, Sunday's from 1pm-5pm.

"Beautiful rolling hills setting. National award winning wines. Written up in Wine Spectator, Wine Enthusiast, and Wine Advocate."

Loew Vineyards

14001 Liberty Road, Mt. Airy, Maryland, 21771   (301)831-5464, www.loewvineyards.net

Wines: Chardonnay, Cabernet, Riesling, Proprietary Blends, Honey Wines, Blueberry Wine.

Tastings/tours available, call for hours.

"We are a boutique winery, family owned and operated. We offer premium, hand crafted wines presented in an intimate atmosphere."

Woodhall Wine Cellars

17912 York Road, Parkton, Maryland, 21120   (410)357-8644, (410)467-8438~Fax, www.woodhallwinecellars.com

Wines: Seyval, Vidal, Chardonnay, Riesling, Cabernet Blanc, Chambourein, Merlot, Cabernet Sarrignon.

Tastings/tours available Tuesdays through Sunday from 12pm-5pm.

Fee of ten dollars per person for groups of ten or more.

"Governor's Cup and thirteen medals, 2000 Maryland Wine judging; located moments from I-83, visit www.woodhallcellars for additional reasons to visit."

Berrywine Plantations/Linganore Winecellars
13601 Glisans Mill Road, Mt. Airy, Maryland, 21771   (410)795-6432,
(301)831-5889, (410)829-1970~Fax

Wines: Table Wines, Fruit, Berry Wine, Honeywine, Linganore.

Tastings/tours available Monday-Friday from 10am-5pm, Saturday's and Sunday's from 12pm-6pm.

Fiore Winery Inc.
3026 Whiteford Road, Pylesville, Maryland, 21132 (410)836-7605,
www.fiorewinery.com

Wines: Table Wines, Cabernet, Chardonnay.

Tastings/tours available Wednesday through Saturday from 10am-5pm. Sunday's from 12pm-5pm.

"Hillside view of valley with flowers/picnic areas and verandas. Good wines, chilled and waiting!"

Basignani Winery, Ltd.
15722 Falls Road, Sparks, Maryland, 21152 (410)472-0703, (410)472-2536~Fax,
www.basignaniwinery.com

Wines: Cabernet Sauvignon, Lorenzino Reserve (Reserve Cabernet Blend), Marisa, Chardonnay, Seyval, Elena, Riesling, Vidal Blush.

Tastings and tours available Wednesday through Saturday from 11:30am-5:30pm, Sundays from 12pm-6pm.

"Basignani is a small family winery dedicated to producing quality unfiltered wines in the beautiful rolling hills of Butler, Maryland.

MISSISSIPPI

Old South Winery
65 South Concord Avenue, Natchez, Mississippi, 39120   (601)445-9924 (601)442-1215~Fax, www.newu.net

Wines: Table Wines, Muscadine Jam.

Tastings/tours available Monday through Saturday from 10am-5pm, Sunday's. 1pm-5pm. Closed Christmas, Easter, and Thanksgiving.

MISSOURI

Augusta Winery

High and Jackson, P.O. Box 8, Augusta, Missouri, 63332   (636)228-4301, (636)228-4683~Fax, www.augusta.com

Wines: Full bodied Dry Reds to Sweet Wines and Vintage Port.

Tastings available Monday-Saturday from 10am-6pm, Sunday from 12pm-6pm. Terrace on property. Snacks, cheese, and crackers available.

"Nestled in rolling hills of Missouri, deep in wine country. Unique town has antiques, and bed and breakfasts."

Montelle at Osage Ridge

Highway 94, P.O. Box 147, Augusta, Missouri, 63332   (636)228-4464, (636)228-4799 ~Fax, www.montelle.com

Wines: Table Wines, Fruit, Berry, Champagne, Sparkling, Vidal Blanc, Vignoles, Seybval Blanc.

Tastings/tours available Monday-Saturday 10am-5:30pm, Sunday 12pm-5:30pm.

Mount Pleasant Winery

5634 High Street, Augusta, Missouri, 63332   (636)482-4419, (800)467-WINE, (636)228-4426~Fax, www.mountpleasantwinery.com

Wines: Table Wine, Champagne, Sparkling Wine, Vidal Blanc, Seyval Blanc, St. Vincent.

Tastings/tours available Monday-Saturday 10am-5:30pm, Sunday 10am-6pm.

Bias Vineyards and Winery

P.O. Box 93, Berger, Missouri, 63014   (573)834-5475, (573)834-2046~Fax, www.biaswinery.com

Wines: Full range of wines from Dry to Sweet.

Tasting/Tours available from Monday-Saturday from 10am-6pm, Sunday 11am-6pm. Winter hours close at 5pm. Snack trays available.

"Our hospitality keeps customers coming back."

Stone Hill Winery-Branson

601 State Highway 165, Branson, Missouri, 65616   (888)926-9463,
(417)334-1942~Fax, www.stonehillwinery.com

Wines: Estate Bottled Norton, Vidal Blanc, Barrel Fermented Seyval, Chardonel,
Seyval, Missouri Champagne, Hermannsberger, Steinberg, Blush, Vignoles, Rose
Montaigne, Golden Rhine, Golden Spumante, Spumante Blush, Pink Catawba,
Concord, Late Harvest Bignoles, Port, Cream Sherry.

Tastings/tours available daily every 15 minutes.

"Great wine, huge gift shop and a free one hour tour that's fun for the whole family.
Historical and humorous."

Missouri Wine Country

7009 Old Highway 66, Cuba, Missouri, 65453   (573)885-2123

Wines: Table Wines, Fruit, Berry, Champagne, Mt. Pleasant, The Abbey, Hermannhof,
Les Bourgeois, Stone Hill.

Tastings/tours available Monday-Saturday from 9am-5:30pm. Sunday's 11am-5:30pm.

Sugar Creek Winery and Vineyards

125 Boone Country Lane, Defiance, Missouri, 63341   (636)987-2400,
(636)987-2051~Fax

Wines: Vidal Blanc, Seyval Blanc, Chardonel, Michael's Signature Red, Chambourcin,
Cynthiana, La Rustica White, Birdlegs Blush, Boone Country White, La Rustica Red,
Peach Hollow, Raspberry Patch, Blackberry Thicket, Signature Port.

Tastings available, call for hours. No tours at this time. Cheese, sausage, bread, available.

"Spectacular view of Missouri River Valley. Inviting, informal atmosphere."

Blumenhof Vineyards Company

P.O. Box 30, State Highway 94, Dutzow, Missouri, 63342   (636)433-2245, (636)433-
5224~Fax, www.blumenhof.com

Wines: Table Wine, Vidal Blanc, Chambourcin, Blumenhof, Missouri

Weinland, Charrette White, Rayon D'Or.

Open for tastings/tours daily, call for hours. Closed major holidays.

Guide to Fine Wines

Thornhill Vineyards Winery

15 East Main, Hartsburg, Missouri, 65039 (573)657-4295, www.thornhillwines.com

Wines: Norton, Vidal, Mead, Ruby Cabernet, Little Flower, Katy Trail Red, Hartsburger, Nouveau, Rose, B's Blush.

Tastings/tours available Monday-Thursday from 11am-6pm, Friday-Saturday 11am-11pm, Sunday's 11am-7pm. Winter hours may vary. Restaurant on premises. Soup, sandwiches, desserts, cheese baskets.

"Friendly, family owned and operated winery. Relax on the deck or the conservatory style tasting room. Wine for all palates!"

Adam Puchta Winery

1947 Frene Creek Road, Hermann, Missouri, 65041   (573)486-5596, (573)486-2361~Fax

Wines: Norton, Vivant, Seyval.

Tastings/tours available Monday-Saturday from 10am-6pm, Sunday 11am-6pm.

Hermannhof

330 East First Street, Hermann, Missouri, 65041   (573)486-5959

Wines: Table Wines, Champagne, Fruit and Berry Wines, Chambourcin, Norton, Vignoles, Hermannhof.

Tastings/tours available Monday-Saturday from 10am-5pm, Sunday's 11am-5pm.

Bristle Ridge Winery

98 Northeast 641, Montserrat, Missouri, 65336   (660)422-5646

Wines: 9 varieties ranging from Dry White to Sweet Red.

Tastings available Monday through Saturday from 10am-5pm, Sunday 11am-5pm. Cheese and crackers available.

"Established in 1979, first winery in Johnson City. Three story building, with spectacular view and patio area. Family owned and operated."

Stone Hill Winery and Restaurant

1110 Stone Hill Highway, Hermann, Missouri, 65041   (800)909-9463, (573)486-3828~Fax, www.stonehillwinery.com

Wines: Estate Bottled Norton, Vidal Blanc, Barrel Fermented Seyval, Chardonel, Seyval, Missouri Champagne, Hermannsberger, Steinberg, Blush, Vignoles, Rose Montaigne, Golden Rhine, Golden Spumante, Spumante Blush, Pink Catawba, Concorde, Late Harvest Vignoles, Port, Cream Sherry.

Tastings/tours available daily every 20 minutes. Adults $1.50, children 12 and under, .50 cents. Restaurant on premises.

"Missouri's largest, oldest and most prestigious winery. Historic cellars, award winning wines, gift shop and restaurant and a spectacular view."

Stonehaus Farms Vineyard and Winery, L.L.C.

24607 Northeast Colbern Road, Lee's Summit, Missouri, 64086 (816)554-8800, (816)524-7703~Fax, www.stonehausfarmswinery.com

Wines: Chardonel, Cynthiana, Concord, Elderberry, Apple, Cherry.

Tastings available: 4 wines free or all wines $2.00. Tasting/tour combination $5.00 per person. Includes sausages, cheese, crackers. Deli on premises with summer sausage, cheese, crackers.

"Family owned winery 20 minutes from Kansas City. Award winning wines. Panoramic view of vineyard and blueberry farm from garden room/patio."

Gloria Winery and Vineyard

11185 Stave Mill Road, Mountain Grove, Missouri, 65711, (417)926-6263

Wines: Estate bottled French hybrid varieties and blends. Selections range from Red to White, in both Sweet and Dry styles.

Tastings available daily from 11am-7pm. Tours available on request.

Gift shop on premises as well as picnic terrace.

"Small family owned and operated winery and vineyard, personal attention, country setting, romantic history on Springfield/Brandon route."

Guide to Fine Wines

Stone Hill Winery-New Florence

485 Booneslick Road, New Florence, Missouri, 63363 (573)835-2420, (573)835-2419~Fax, www.stonehillwinery.com

Wines: Estate Bottled Norton, Vidal Blanc, Barrel Fermented Seyval, Chardonei, Seyval, Missouri Champagne, Hermannsberger, Steinberg, Blush, Vignoles, Rose Montaigne, Golden Rhine, Golden Spumante, Spumante Blush, Pink Catawba, Concord, Late Harvest Vignoles, Port, Cream Sherry.

Tastings/tours available daily, call for hours.

"Conveniently located off I-70. Travelers can run in for purchase or linger in gift shop and sample award winning wines."

Ferrigno Vineyards and Winery

17301 State Route B, Saint James, Missouri, 65559 (573)265-7742, www.ferigno@fidnet.com

Wines: Ten wines ranging from Dry to Sweet.

Tastings/tours available Monday through Saturday from 10am-6pm, Sunday's from 12pm-6pm. Picnic foods and picnic area available.

"Family operated, hand crafted wines of quality and character."

Sainte Genevieve Winery

245 Merchant Street, Sainte Genevieve, Missouri, 63670   (573)483-2012

Wines: Table Wine, Fruit, Berry Wines.

Tastings/tours available Sunday-Saturday from 11am-5pm.

Les Bourgeois Vineyards, Inc.

I-70 and Route BB, Rocheport, Missouri, 65279   (573)698-2133, (573)698-2174~Fax, www.missouriwine.com

Wines: Full variety of wines.

Tastings/tours available daily from 11am-6pm. Large groups by reservation.
Restaurant on premises.

"One of mid-Missouri's premier recreational and cultural attractions. Award-winning wine, exquisite bistro cuisine, and a spectacular view."

Winery of the Little Hills

501 South Main Street, Saint Charles, Missouri, 63301   (636)946-9165,
(636)724-1121~Fax, www.little-hills.com

Wines: Table, Fruit, and Berry Wines.

Tastings/tours available Monday-Thursday from 11am-9pm, Saturday's and Sunday's
11am-11pm.

Saint James Winery

540 Sidney Street, Saint. James, Missouri, 65559   (573)265-7912, (573)265-6200~Fax

Wines: Table Wine, Champagne, Sparkling Wine, Fruit Wine, Grape Juice, Vignoles,
Norton, Seyval.

Tastings/tours available Monday-Saturday from 8am-7pm, Sunday 11am-7pm.

Peaceful Bend Vineyard, L.L.C.

1942 Highway T, Steelville, Missouri, 65565   (573)775-300, (573)775-3001~Fax,
www.peacefulbendvineyard.com

Wines: Full range of White and Red wines from Dry to Sweet.

Tastings available Tuesday-Friday from 10am-5pm, Saturday from 10am-6pm,
Sunday's from 12pm-5pm. Tours by appointment. Snack trays, cheese, wine and
sausage available.

"Great wine, beautiful scenery. Hiking trails, cottage, and relaxation for all our visitors."

Pirtle Winery

502 Spring, Weston, Missouri, 64098   (816)640-5728, (816)386-5319~Fax,
www.pirtlewine.com

Wines: Reds (Norton, St. Vincent), Whites (Sequal, Cayuga, Delaware), Apple wine,
Meads (Honey wine), Blackberry Mead, Raspberry Mead, Sparkling Mead.

Tastings available from 10am-6pm daily. Restaurant on premises.

"Visit our tasting room housed in an 1867 church. Enjoy wines in serene wine garden
for a relaxing picnic."

Guide to Fine Wines

Heinrichshaus Vineyards and Winery
18500 State Route U, Saint James, Missouri, 65559   (573)265-5000

Wines: Table Wines, Vidal Blanc, Cynthiana, Chambourcin, Heinrichshaus.

Tastings/tours available daily except Wednesday. Call for hours.

Buffalo Creek Winery
29003 Possum Trot Road, Stover, Missouri, 65078   (573)377-4535,
(573)377-4535~Fax, www.buffalocreekwinery.com

Wines: Red, White, and Fruit wines including Persimmon.

Tastings/tours available Monday-Saturday from 10am-6pm, Sunday from 11am-7pm.
Winter hours from 10am-5pm. Picnic foods available such as sausage and smoked
trout.

"Free shuttle from boat ramp to winery. Only winery on Lake of the Ozarks. Great
food and cabin for rent."

La Dolce Vita Vineyard and Winery
72 Forest Hills Drive, Washington, Missouri 63090   (636)239-0399,
(636)239-7279~Fax, www.ladolcevitawinery.com

Wines: Cynthiana.

Tastings/tours available by appointment.

"La Dolce Vita produces 400 cases a year of 100% Cynthiana wine. (Missouri's best
red). Bed and Breakfast accommodations available."

NEW MEXICO

La Chiripada Winery
Highway 75, Dixon, New Mexico, 87527   (505)579-4437, (505)579-4437~Fax

Wines: Table Wine, Port.

Tastings/tours available Monday-Saturday 10am-5pm, Sunday's 12pm-5pm.

Anderson Valley Vineyards

4920 Rio Grande Boulevard North West, Albuquerque, New Mexico, 87107
(505)344-7266, (505)345-7748~Fax

Wines: Chardonnay, Cabernet Sauvignon, White Zinfandel, Johannisberg Riesling,
Claret, Burgundy, and unique specialties such as Balloon Blush and Red Chili Wine.

Tours and tastings available. Call for times and varying fees. Gift shop on premise,
open Tuesday through Sunday, call to confirm hours.

"Large variety of award winning wines. One of the largest New Mexico wineries.
Founded by Maxie L. Anderson family."

Casa Rondena Winery

733 Chavez Road North West, Albuquerque, New Mexico, 87107 (505)344-5911,
(505)343-1823~Fax, www.casarondena.com

Wines: Cabernet Franc, Chardonnay, Riesling.

Tastings/tours available Tuesday-Sunday from 10am-6pm.

"Beautiful winery and vineyards creating a gracious environment, and offering some of
New Mexico's most unique architecture."

Gruet Winery

8400 Pan American North East, Albuquerque, New Mexico, 87113 (505)821-0055,
(888)857-WINE, (505)857-0066~Fax, www.gruetwinery.com

Wines: Sparkling Wines: Brut, Blanc de Noirt, Blanc de Blancs, Demi-sec, Rose'. Stiff
Wines: Chardonnay, Chardonnay "Barrel Select", Pinot Noir.

Tastings/tours available Monday through Friday from 10am-5pm, Saturdays from
12pm-5pm. $5.00 fee per person, includes wine glass.

"Gruet winery has it's origins in Champagne, France and specializes in sparkling
wines. Also produces some excellent Chardonnays and Pinot Noir."

Guide to Fine Wines

San Felipe Winery
2011 Mountain Road, Albuquerque, New Mexico, 87104 (505)843-8171, (505)843-8107~Fax

Wines: Table Wines, Champagne, Sparkling Wine, Merlot, Cabernet Sauvignon.

Tastings/tours available daily from 12pm-5pm, closed Tuesday's.

Sandia Shadows Vineyard and Winery
11704 Coronado North East #14, Albuquerque, New Mexico, 87122 (505)856-1006, (505)858-0859~Fax

Wines: Table Wine, Fruit and Berry Wines, Green and Red Chile Wine, Chardonnay, Sauvignon Blanc, Cabernet Sauvignon, Sandia Shadows.

Tastings/tours available Monday-Saturday from 12pm-5pm.

New Mexico Wineries, INC.
P.O. Box 1180, Deming, New Mexico, 88031   (505)546-9324, (505)546-7905~Fax, www.zianet.com/nmwineries

Wines: Table Wine, Champagne, Sparkling Wine, Cabernet Sauvignon, Merlot, Chardonnay, Blue Teal, Mademoiselle, St. Clair, D.H. Lescombes.

Tastings/tours available daily from 10am-6pm.

La Vina Winery
4201 South Highway 28, La Union, New Mexico, 88021   (505)882-7632, (505)882-7632~Fax, lavingstar@aol.com

Wines: Broad range- Dry Red and White to Sparkling Muscat and Port.

Tastings available daily from 12pm-5pm.

Tours daily at 11:30am. $5.00 fee per person for tour, $2.00 fee for tastings.

"Visit New Mexico's oldest winery along the Juan De Onate trail. Sample great wines as America's oldest wine growing region continues it's traditions in wine making."

Santa Fe Vineyards

Route 1, Box 216A, Espanola, New Mexico, 87532   (505)753-8100, (505)753-8100~Fax, www.nmwine.net

Wines: Chardonnay, Sauvignon Blanc, Indian Market White, Merlow, Zinfandel, Cabernet.

Tastings and tours available in tasting room. Gift shop on premises as well as outdoor picnic area. Call for hours.

"We feature many award winning wines and a southwestern oriented gift shop. Our labels are original paintings by Amado M. Pena, Jr."

Anasazi Fields Winery

P.O. Box 712, 26 Camino De Los Puebcitos, Placitas, New Mexico, 87043 (505)867-3062, (505)867-8539~Fax, www.nmwine.net/anasazi

Wines: Apricot, Peach, Cherry, Plum, Raspberry, Cranberry.

Tastings/tours available on Saturdays from 10am-5pm, and Sunday 12pm-5pm. Other times by appointment.

"Fine dry table wines handcrafted from fresh fruits and berries-most locally grown. No sweet wines."

Black Mesa Winery

1502 Highway 68, Velarde, New Mexico, 87582   (800)852-6372, (800)852-6372~Fax, www.blackmesawinery.com

Wines: Chardonnay, Cabernet Sauvignon, Fume Blanc, Merlot, Sangiovese, Dolcheto, Riesling

Tastings/tours available Monday through Saturday from 10am-6pm, and Sundays from 12pm-6pm.

"Located in northern New Mexico on main road between Santa Fe and Taos. Wines made using New Mexico grapes. RV parking."

Madison
Star Route 490, Ribera, New Mexico, 87560, (505)421-8028, (505)421-8028~Fax, www.madisonwinery.com

Wines: Baco, Seyval.

Tastings/tours available Monday-Saturday from 10am-5pm.

"Hand crafted wines that are very good."

Ponderosa Valley Winery
3171 Highway 290, Ponderosa, New Mexico, 87044 (505)834-7073, (505)834-7073~Fax, www.ponderosawinery.com

Wines: Zinfandel, Pinot Noir, Merlot, Cabernet Sauvignon, Chardonnay, Sauvignon Blanc, Dry Riesling, Chenin Blanc, Summer Sage, Jemez blush, NM Riesling, Chemisa Gold, Late Harvest Riesling.

Tastings and tours are available. Call for times.

"The winery is nestled in an open valley of the Jemez mountains. All of our wines are award winners and we strive to find the wine you like."

Tularosa Vineyards
23 Coyote Canyon Road, Rularosa, New Mexico, 88352   (505)585-2260, (505)585-2260~Fax, www.tularosavineyards.com

Wines: Cabernet Sauvignon, Merlot, Sangiovese, Syrah, Gewürztraminer, Sauvignon Blanc, et. al..

Tastings/tours available daily from 12pm-5pm.

"Classic varietal wines from New Mexico. A refreshing change from California wine."

NORTH CAROLINA
Dennis Vineyards, Inc.
24043 Endy Road, Albemayle, North Carolina, 28001 (704)982-6090

Wines: Table Wines, Carlos, Noble.

Tastings/tours available by appointment.

Biltmore Estate Wine Company

One North Pack Square, Asheville, North Carolina, 28801 (828)274-6214.

Wines: Table Wines, Champagne, Chardonnay, Cabernet Sauvignon, White Zinfandel.

Tastings/tours available Monday-Saturday 11am-6pm, Sunday 12pm-6pm.

Germanton

Route 1, Box 1-G, Germanton, North Carolina, 27019   (336)969-2075,
www.germantongallery.com

Wines: Seybal, Niagara.

Tastings/tours available Tuesday-Friday 10am-6pm, Saturday's 9am-5pm. Call for hours on Sunday's.

Martin Vineyards

Route 1256, 213 Martin Farm Lane, Knotts Island, North Carolina, 27950 (252)429-3542, (252)429-3564, (252)429-3095~Fax, www.martinvineyards.com

Wines: Merlot, Cabernet Sauvignon, Atlantis Red, Vioquier, Chardonnay, Muscadine, Apple, Strawberry, Fruitville White.

Tastings/tours available seven days per week from 12pm-6pm.

"88 acre estate. Maritime climate with ocean breezes and sandy soil. Spectacular views from our picnic grounds on Knotts Island Bay."

Westbend Vineyards

5394 Williams Road, Lewisville, North Carolina, 27023   (336)945-5032,
(336)945-5294~Fax, www.ncwine.org

Wines: Chardonnay, Merlot, Viognier, Cabernet Sauvignon, Riesling, Muscat, Canelli.

Call for information on tastings/tours.

"Produced from our 70 acre prime vineyards. Acclaimed and nationally recognized for quality. Truly a homegrown product from this region"

Guide to Fine Wines

Bennett Vineyards, LTD.
6832 Bonnerton Road, Edward, North Carolina, 27821 (252)322-7154,
www.ncwines.com

Wines: Table Wines.

Tastings/tours available daily. Call for hours.

Duplin Wine Cellars
Highway 117, Rose Hill, North Carolina, 28458   (910)289-3888, (800)774-9634,
(910)289-3094~Fax, www.duplinwinery.com

Wines: Table Wines, Champagne, Sparkling Wine.

Tastings/tours available Monday-Saturday 9am-5pm.

N.C. Waldensian Wines
1530 19th Street South West, Rose Hill, North Carolina, 28602 (828)327-3867,
www.waldensian.com

Wines: Table Wines, Champagne, Sparkling Wine, Sparkling non-alcoholic Ciders,
Scuppermong, Muscadine.

Tastings/tours available, but call for hours first.

The Teensy Winery
3661 Painters Gap, Union Mills, North Carolina, 28167 (828)287-7763,
(828)287-7763~Fax

Wines: Table Wines, Chardonnay, Cabernet Sauvignon, Merlot.

Tastings/tours available by appointment.

Waldensian Heritage Wines
4940 Vallar Lane North East, Valdese, North Carolina, 28690, (828)879-3202

Wines: Table Wines.

Tastings/tours available Friday-Sunday 1pm-6pm.

Shelton Vinyards, Inc.
286 Cabernet Lane, Dobson North Carolina, 27017 (336) 366-4724 (336) 366-4758
www.sheltonvineyards.com

Wines: NC Chardonnay, Georgia Black Stock Vineyards Viognier, madison Lee Blend, Syrah, NC Merlot, GA BlackStock Vineyards Merlot, NC Cabernet Sauvignon, Salem Fork Blush

Tasting/Tours: $5 per person, Monday-Saturday 10 am-5pm, Sunday 1-5 pm.

OUr 300 acre vineyard and winery offers estate grown and bottled wines as well as handmade artisan style cheeses.

Hanover Park Vineyard
1927 Courtney-Huntsville Road, Yadkinville, North Carolina, 27055 (336)463-2875, (336)463-2875~Fax, www.hanoverparkwines.com

Wines: Cabernet Sauvignon, Cabernet Franc, Chambourcin, Mouvedre, Chardonnay, Viogne, Rose.

Tastings/tours available on Thursday's and Friday's from 4pm-6pm, Saturday's 12pm-6pm, and Sunday's from 1pm-5pm. Summer hours on Thursday's and Friday's are from 12pm-6pm.

"1887 restored farm house under majestic oaks with picnic areas. Customers say this is the best wine in North Carolina!"

OKLAHOMA

Cimarron Cellars
Route 1, Box 79, Caney, Oklahoma, 74533 (580)889-5997, (580)889-6312~Fax
Wines: Variety of Whites, Blushes, Reds, and Fruit Wines.
Tastings available Monday-Saturday 12pm-5pm. Tours by appointment.
"We were the first commercial Vineyard and Winery in Oklahoma."

Robert Bartunek Winery
1920 South Cleveland, Enid, Oklahoma, 73703 (580)233-6337, (580)233-2513~Fax
Wines: Table Wines, Wine Jelly, Chenin Blanc, Muscat Blanc, Cabernet Sauvignon.
Tastings/tours Friday and Saturday's 1pm-5pm, or by appointment.

Guide to Fine Wines

Tres Suenos Winery

19691 E. Charter Oak Road, Luther, Oklahoma, 73054   (405)277-7089, (405)373-3626~Fax

Wines: Blush, Oklahoma Select White, Muscat Cannelli, Chenin Blanc, Chardonnay, Charter Oak Red, Anniversary Red Reserve, Riesling.

Tastings/tours available. Call for hours.

"Great rural setting-great wines, great festivals-meet the wine maker and have a glass of wine with him."

SOUTH CAROLINA

Montmorenci Vineyards

110 Old Dibble Road, Aiken, South Carolina, 29801 (803)649-4870, (803)642-1834~Fax

Wines: Table Wines, Champagne, Melody, Cayuga White, Chambourcin.

Tastings/tours available Wednesday-Saturday 10am-6pm. Closed first two weeks in January.

Windy Hill Orchard

1860 Highway 5, York, South Carolina, 29745   (803)684-0690, (803)684-6814~Fax

Wines: Apple.

Tastings/tours available Monday-Saturday from 9am-6pm.

"Unique hard cider. Also unique to the old English district that we live in."

TENNESSEE

Tennessee Mountain View Winery

352 Union Grove Road, North East, Charleston, Tennessee, 37310 (423)479-7311

Wines: Table Wines, Fruit, Berry, Scuppermong, Catawaba, Concord.

Tastings/tours daily from 12pm-6pm.

Countryside Vineyards Winery

658 Henry Harr Road, Blountville, Tennessee, 37617   (423)323-1660,
www.cvwineryandsupply.com

Wines: Dry Vidal, Chardonnay, Semi-Dry Vidal, Steuben, Blush, Countryside White, Niagara, Golden Muscat, Just Peachy, Muscadine, Chambourcin, Chambourcin Nouveau, Leon Millot, Spaghetti Red, Countryside Red, Autumn Harvest, Blackberry.

Tastings/tours available any time, as long as owners available. Call first.

"We are family owned and operated with a wide variety of wines. Stop by and taste our award-winning wines."

Beachaven Vineyards and Winery

1100 Dunlop Lane, Clarksville, Tennessee, 37040   (931)645-8867,
(931)645-3522~Fax, www.beachavenwinery.com

Wines: Chardonnay, Merlot, Cabernet Sauvignon, Riesling, Blackberry, Port.

Complimentary tastings/tours available. Call for hours.

"Our family owned and operated winery features French-method Champagnes, award winning wines, and an extensive gift shop."

Lowe's Winery

136 Forrest Hill Road, Cookeville, Tennessee 38506   (931)498-4014

Wines: Apple, Apple Mead, Apricot, Apricot Mead, Beet, Blackberry, Blueberry, Cabernet Sanvignon, Chamblaise, Cherry, Concord, Cranberry, Elderberry, Emerald Reisling, Gamay Noir, Muscadine Rose, Muscadine White, Orange Blossom Mead, Peach, Pinot Noir, Rasberry, Red Grape, Reliance Blush, Sauvignon Blanc, Spring Ridge Blend, Strawberry, Thomas White, Vinegar Blackberry, Watermelon, Zinfandel Blush, Zinfandel Red.

"A mom and pop operation with nothing fancy. No cheese, restaurant or antiques. 24 flavors always on hand, something for everyone."

Guide to Fine Wines

Cordova Cellars, INC.
9050 Macon Road, Cordova, Tennessee, 38088   (901)754-3442, (901)755-9612~Fax

Wines: Table Wines, Muscadine, Venus, Cabernet Sauvignon.

Tastings/tours available Tuesday-Saturday 10am-5pm, Sunday's 1pm-5pm.

Chestnut Hill Winery
78 Chestnut Hill Road, Crossville, Tennessee, 38555   (931)707-5656, (931)707-7372~Fax

Wines: Table Wines

Tastings/tours available daily from 9am-9pm.

Stonehaus Winery
2444 Genesis Road, Crossville, Tennessee, 38558   (931)484-9463, (931)484-9425~Fax, www.stonehauswinery.com

Wines: Chardonnay, Pleasant Hilll Red, Homestead White, Lantana White, Davenport Red, Helena Blush, Miscadine, Rasberry Mist, Cumberland Gold and Orange Squeeze.

Tastings/tours available. Call for hours.

"Stonehaus has one of the largest wine tasting rooms in America. A gourmet restaurant, deli, cheese/gift shop and an antique mall."

Long Hollow Winery
665 Long Hollow Pike, Goodlettsville, Tennessee, 37073 (615)859-8844, (615)859-5559~Fax

Table Wines, Fruit, Berry, Sacramental Wines.

Tastings/tours available Monday-Saturday 7am-7pm.

Smoky Mountain Winery, INC.
450 Cherry Street, Suite 2, Gatlinburg, Tennessee, 37738   (865)436-7551, (865)436-0584~Fax, www.smokymountainwinery.com

Wines: Table Wines, Fruit Berry, Sparkling Wines.

Tastings/tours available daily starting at 10am year round.

Highland Manor Winery, Inc.

2965 South York Highway, Jamestown, Tennessee 38556 (931)879-9519, (931)879-2907~Fax

Wines: Seyval Blanc, Chardonnay, Highland Red, Cabernet Sauvignon, Royal White, White Riesling, Highland Sunset, Cayuga White, Royal Rose', Muscadine, Southern Blush.

Tastings/tours are available as well as wine and cheese picnics.

"Highland Manor is the oldest winery in Tennessee. All of our wines are award winners. We give personal guided tours."

Loudon Valley Vineyards

555 Huff Ferry Road North, Loudon, Tennessee, 37771 (865)986-8736,

Wines: Table Wines, Fruit, Berry, Chardonnay, Riesling, Muscadine.

Tastings/tours available Monday-Saturday 10am-6pm, Sunday's 1pm-5pm.

Tennessee Valley Wine Corp.

15606 Hotchkiss Valley Road East, Loudon, Tennessee, 37774 (615)986-5147

Wines: Table Wine, Fruit, Berry, Muscadine, Vidal Blanc, Concord.

Tastings/tours available Monday-Saturday 10am-6pm, Sunday's 1pm-5pm.

Marlow Wine Cellars, INC.

(dba Monteagle Wine Cellars)

P. O Box 638, Monteagle, Tennessee, 37356   (931)924-2120, (800)556-WINE, (931)924-2587~Fax

Wines: Table Wine, Fruit, Berry, Riesling, Gewürztraminer, Cabernet Sauvignon.

Tastings/tours available April-October Monday-Saturday from 8am-6pm, Sunday's 12pm-5pm. November-March hours are Monday-Saturday 9am-5pm, Sunday's 12pm-5pm.

Guide to Fine Wines

Orr Mountain Winery

355 Pumpkin Hollow Road, Madisonville, Tennessee, 37354 (423)442-5340

Wines: Tellico Rose, Celebration, Festival Gold, Bald River Red, Chardonnay.

Complimentary tastings available. Call for hours.

"We have a lovely setting in the country, with a view of the mountains and a picnic area. Our wines are great!"

Mountain Valley Vineyards, INC.

2174 Parkway, Pigeon Forge, Tennessee, 37863 (865)453-6334,
(865)428-4052~Fax

Wines: Table Wines, Fruit, Berry, Muscadine.

Tastings/tours Monday-Saturday 10am-6pm, Sunday's 12pm-6pm.

Sumner Crest Winery

5306 Old Highway 52, Portland, Tennessee 37148 (615)325-4086,
(615)325-6360~Fax sumnercrestwinery.com

Wines: Cabernet Sauvignon, Merlot, Chardonnay, Sequal Vidal, Niagra Concord, Muscadine, Blackberry, Reisling, Champagne, Port, many others.

Tastings daily from 9am-5pm. Tours at 12pm, 2pm and 4pm or by appointment.

"Internationally awarded wines. Antique cars, European antiques, remarkable gift shop, monthly outdoor musical events."

Lauderdale Cellars Winery and Vineyard

1900 Highway 51 South, Ripley, Tennessee, 38063 (731)635-4321,
(731)635-7678~Fax, www.lauderdalecellars.com

Wines: Cabernet Sauvignon, Merlot, Tennessee Red, Oasis, Vidal Red Garnet, Blue Velvet, Blackberry Winder, Ambrosia, White Muscadine, Niagara.

Tastings/tours available daily. Call for information.

"Produce fine wines, ranging from full-bodied reds to sweet whites. Visit the largest vineyard in Tennessee for an unforgettable experience."

Apple Barn Winery
220 Apple Valley Road, Sevierville, Tennessee, 37862 (865)428-6850,
(865)428-4052~Fax

Wines: Table Wines, Fruit, Berry.

Tours/tastings available daily from 9am-6pm.

Tri-Star Vineyards and Winery
168 Scales Road, Shelbyville, Tennessee, 37160   (931)294-3062

Wines: Baconoir, Foch, Cayuga, Chancellor, Rosette, Catawba, Blended Grapes, Red and White Muscadine, Fruit and Berry Wines.

Tastings are available, call for schedule.

"Small family owned winery nestled in the heart of Tennessee Walking Horse country."

TEXAS

Cana Cellars Winery
11217 Fitzhugh Road, Austin, Texas, 78736   (512)288-6027, (515)474-8252~Fax

Wines: Cabernet Sauvignon, Merlow, Chardonnay, Fume Blanc, Muscat Canille, Cabernet Rose.

Tastings/tours available Saturday and Sunday from 12pm-5pm, or by appointment. Small retail gift shop on premises.

"Located in the cellar of Joe and Deena Turner's house in Texas Hill country. You'll be greeted by grazing long horn!"

Hill Country Cellars
1700 North Bell, Cedar Park, Texas, 78613   (512)259-2000, (512)259-2092~Fax

Wines: Table Wines, Champagne, Sparkling Wine, Chardonnay, Cabernet Sauvignon, Sauvignon Blanc.

Tastings available daily from 12pm-5pm. Tours at 1pm daily. Friday-Sunday tours also available at 2pm, 3pm, and 4pm, or by appointment.

Messina Hof Winery and Resort

4545 Old Reliance Road, Bryan, Texas, 77840   (979)778-9463, (800)736-9463, (979)778-1729~Fax, www.messinahof.com

Wines: Blush, White Zinfandel, Chenin Blanc, Johannisberg Riesling, Rose Gamay Beaujolais, Semmillon, Muscat, Canelli, Sauvignon Blanc, Pinot Grigio, Cabernet Sauvignon, Merlot, Pinot Noir, Shiraz, Chardonnay.

Tastings available Monday-Friday from 8:30am-5:30pm, Saturday's 10am-5pm,

Sunday's 12pm-4pm. Tours available Monday-Friday at 1pm and 2:30pm, Saturday at 11am, 12:30pm, 2:30pm, and 4pm, Sunday at 12:30pm and 2:30pm. $5.00 fee for regular tour. $7.00 fee for private tour. "The Vintage House" restaurant on premises.

"Messina Hof-Texas' most unique wine experience. Luxury villa. Vineyard view restaurant. Texas' most awarded wines."

Sister Creek Vineyard

1142 Sisterdale Road, Boerne, Texas, 78006   (830)324-6704, (830)324-6704~Fax, www.sistercreekvineyards.com

Wines: Chardonnay, Pinot Noir, Cabernet (3 varieties), Merlot, Specialty House Wine Muscat Canelli.

Tastings/tours available daily from 12pm-5pm. No fee. Those desiring to keep special glass pay $3.00.

"Set in cotton gin from 1885. Some original equipment. Scenic creek on grounds. Hill country between Fredricksburg and Boerne."

Pleasant Hill Winery

1441 Salem Road, Brenham, Texas, 77833   (979)830-8463,

Wines: Table Wines.

Tours/tastings available Saturday's 11am-6pm, and Sunday's 12pm-5pm.

La Bodega Winery

Dallas-Fort Worth International Airport, Terminal A, Gate A15, DFW Airport, Texas 75261
(972)574-6208, (972)574-4353~Fax, www.labodegawinery.com

Wines: La Bodega Winery Private Reserve Merlot 1997, La Bodega Winery Private Reserve Cabernet Sauvignon 1998, La Bodega Winery Private Reserve Chardonnay 1999, and Texas County Blush.

Tastings available, wines by the glass, 20 varieties of Texas wines/bottles and cases for sale plus wine related gifts. $4-9 fee for tastings/wine by the glass. Light snack foods available.

"La Bodega Winery, "The World's First Winery in an Airport". Creates a one of a kind experience for the traveling wine connoisseur."

Val Verde Winery

100 Qualia Drive, Del Rio, Texas, 78840   (830)775-9714, (830)775-5394~Fax

Wines: Chardonnay, Sauvignon Blanc, Muscat Canelli, Texas Rose, Merlot, Cabernet Sauvignon, and Tawny Port.

Tastings/tours available daily from 10am-5pm. Large groups by appointment.

"Third generation Texas wine maker, since 1883. Family owned hand made wines in the old world Italian tradition."

Ste. Genevieve Wines, Escondido Valley Wines

IH 10 Exit 285, Fort Stockton, Texas 79735   (915)395-2417, (915)395-2431~Fax

Wines: Ste Genevieve-Cabernet, Sauvignon, Chardonnay, Zinfandel, Sauvignon Blanc, Texas Red, Texas White, Texas Blush, Gamay Frame Chardonnay, Merlot. Escondido Valley-Syrah, Pinot Noir, Chardonnay, Cabernet Sauvignon, Merlot.

Tastings/tours are conducted by the City of Fort Stockton Tourism Division. Call for information at :(800)334-8525, (915)336-8052, (915)336-8525. Tours include transportation from Fort Stockton. $8.00 fee per adult.

"Ste. Genevieve Wines is the largest winery and vineyard operation in Texas. We are located among ruggedly beautiful desert mesas in west Texas."

Guide to Fine Wines

Bell Mountain Vineyards

463 Bell Mountain Road, Fredricksburg, Texas, 78624   (830)685-3297,
(830)685-3657~Fax, www.bellmountainwine.com

Wines: Premium Wines including Blended, Cabernet, Chardonnay, Reisling and others.

Tastings and tours available Saturdays from 10am-5pm. Other times by appointment.
Picnic grounds available.

"Located in charming German community. 56 acres of beautiful grounds with German
architecture. Wines made from all our own grapes."

La Buena Vida Vineyards

416 East College Street, Grapevine, Texas, 76051   (817)481-9463,
(817)421-3635~Fax, www.labuenavida.com

Wines: Tx Champagne, Tx Ports, Tx Chardonnay, Tx Cabernet Sauvignon, Tx
Sauvignon Blanc, Tx White Zinfandel, Tx White Merlot, Tx Merlot, Chile Merlot, Chile
Chardonnay.

Tastings/tours available Monday-Saturday from 10am-5pm, Sunday's from 12pm-5pm.
$7.00 fee per person for four tastings and souvenir glass. Picnic area on premises.

"Charming limestone former church in historic district. Native Texas gardens, foun-
tains, herb garden and Texas winery museum. Wisteria covered arbors."

Delaney Vineyards

2000 Champagne Boulevard, Grapevine, Texas, 76051 (817)481-5668,
(817)251-8119~Fax, www.delaneyvineyards.com

Wines: Cabernet Sauvignon, Merlot, Sparkling Wine, Sauvignon Blanc, Muscat
Cannelli, Barrel Fermented Chardonnay, Texas Rose.

Tours available daily at no charge. $7.51 charge for tastings. Call for hours.

Has second location in Lamesa, Texas. Call for information.

"18th century French chateau styled winery with old world ambiance and rustic ele-
gance. Site on 28 acres in Dallas/Fort Worth area.

Fredericksburg Winery

247 West Main, Fredericksburg, Texas, 78624   (830)990-8747, (830)990-8566~Fax, www.fbgwinery.com

Wines: Table Wines, Champagne, Sparkling Wine, Cabernet Sauvignon, Orange Muscat, Chardonnay.

Tastings/tours available Monday-Thursday 10am-6pm, Friday's and Saturday's 10am-8pm, Sunday 12pm-6pm.

Texas Hills Vineyard

878 Rural Route 2766, Johnson City, Texas 78636   (830)868-2321, (830)868-7027~Fax, www.texashillsvineyard.com

Wines: Chardonnay, Pinot Grigio, Sangiovese, Merlot Cabernet Sauvignon, Cabernet Franc, Tre Paesyno Moscato.

Tastings and tours available Monday through Saturday from 10am-5pm. Sundays from 12pm-5pm. Fee of $3.00 for premium wine tasting.

"A "Texas-friendly" tasting room with wines in an Italian accent. Texas wines in the style of Italy."

Cap Rock Winery

A mile east of U.S. 87 on Woodrow Road, Lubbock, Texas, 79423 (806)863-2704, (800)546-WINE, (806)863-2712~Fax, www.caprockwinery.com

Wines: Table Wine, Champagne, Sparkling Wines.

Tastings/tours available Monday-Saturday 10am-5pm, Sunday's 12pm-5pm.

Llano Estacado Winery

(Staked Plains)

FM 1585, Lubbock, Texas, 79452   (806)745-2258, (806)748-1674~Fax

Wines: Table Wines, Champagne, Cabernet Sauvignon, Chardonnay, Sauvignon Blanc.

Tastings/tours available Monday-Saturday 10am-4pm, Sunday's 12pm-4pm.

Pheasant Ridge Winery

Route 3, Box 191, Lubbock, Texas 79401   (806)746-6033, (806)746-6750~Fax, www.pheasantridgewinery.com

Wines: Cabernet Sauvignon, Merlot, Pinot Noir, Prop. Res., Chardonnay, and Dry Chenin Blanc.

Tastings and tours available by appointment.

"Pheasant Ridge wines are 100% estate grown and the fruit is hand picked from our 65 acres of vineyard."

Piney Woods Country Wines

3408 Willow Drive, Orange, Texas, 77632 (409)883-5408, (409)883-5483~Fax

Wines: Four Fruit Wines, seven Muscadine Grape Wines including two Light Ports and two Sparkling Wines.

Tastings available Monday-Saturday from 9am-5pm. Self-guided vineyard tours for adults. Winery tours are for groups, and are by appointment only for a small fee.

"We are a small winery and our wines are different-most on the sweet fruity side-all are award winners."

Hidden Springs Winery

256 North Highway 377, Pilot Point, Texas 76258   (940)686-2782, (940)686-4206~Fax, www.hiddenspringswinery.com

Wines: Sauvignon Blanc, Cabernet Sauvignon, Chardonnay and other varieties.

Tastings/tours available from Tuesday through Saturday, 12pm-5pm. Gift shop with crafts on premise, as well as gourmet foods available.

"Hidden Springs is a study in Victorian warmth, beauty and charm. Features include a turn or the century oak bar and Victorian decor."

Blum Street Cellars

849 East Commerce #200F, San Antonio, Texas, 78205 (210)222-BLUM, (210)226-WINE

Tastings/tours available Monday-Thursday 9:30am-9:30pm, Friday and Saturday from 9:30am-10:30pm, Sunday's 10am-8pm. Call for information on available products.

Homestead Vineyards and Winery, INC.

Vineyard Lane, Ivanhoe, Texas, 75447   (903)583-4281, Tasting Room located at 220 West Main, Davison, Texas, 75020.

Wines: Table Wines, Merlot, Cabernet Sauvignon, Muscat Canelli.

Tasting room open to guests Wednesday-Saturday 11am-6pm.

Poteet Country Winery

400 Tank Hollow Road, Poteet, Texas, 78065   (830)276-8085 (830)742-8274~Fax, www.poteetwine.com

Wines: Strawberry, Blackberry, Mustang, White Mustang, Peach, Pear.

Tastings/tours available Friday-Sunday from 12pm-6pm. Chuck Wagon on premises.

"A stay in the country, picnics, windmills, cows, and even old chuck wagons are all part of the Poteet Country experience."

Spicewood Vineyards

1423 C R 409, Spicewood, Texas, 78669   (830)693-5328, (830)693-5940~Fax, www.spicewoodvineyards.com

Wines: Sauvignon Blanc, Chardonnay, Merlot, Cabernet Sauvignon, Blush.

Tastings/tours most weekends from 1pm-4pm, call first. $3.00 fee per person.

"All wines are made from grapes grown at our vineyard in the heart of the Texas Hill Country."

Red River Winery

421 Gentry Street #204, Spring, Texas, 77373 (281)288-9463, (281)288-9463~Fax, www.redriverwinery.com

Wines: Ruby Cabernet, Cabernet Sauvignon, Merlot, Pinot Noir, Chenin Blanc, Blush, Chardonnay.

Wine tastings available all day, call for hours.

"We offer personalized wine labels, great for birthdays, weddings, corporate gifts or any special occasion."

Becker Vineyards

464 Becker Farms Road, Stonewall, Texas, 78671 (830)644-2681, (830)644-2689~Fax, www.beckervineyards.com

Wines: 16 different varietals. Chardonnay, Merlot, Cabernet Sauvignon, Riesling, Syvan, Sauvignon Blanc.

Tastings available Monday-Saturday from 10am-5pm, Sunday's 12pm-5pm. Tours available on the hour and the half hour. Fee of $1.50 per person for group tours.

"Replica of German limestone barn situated near vineyards and lavender fields. Handcrafted in Bordeaux and Rhone style of wine making."

Grape Creek Vineyard, INC.

U.S. Highway 290 @ South Grape Creek, Stonewall, Texas, 78671 (830)644-2710, (830)644-2746~Fax

Wines: Table Wines, Cabernet Sauvignon, Chardonnay, Sauvignon Blanc.

Tastings/tours available Monday-Saturday 10am-5pm, Sunday's 12pm-5pm.

Fall Creek Vineyards

1820 C R 222, Tow, Texas, 76862 (512)476-4477, (512)476-6116~Fax, www.fcv.com

Wines: Chardonnay, Chenin Blanc, Merlot, Sauvignon.

Tastings/tours available Monday-Friday from 11am-4pm, Saturday's 12pm-5pm, Sunday's 12pm-4pm. Picnic area on premises.

"Unique combination of soil and micro climate in beautiful hill country of Texas that is producing first class wines."

VIRGINIA

Afton Mountain Vineyards

234 Vineyard Lane, Afton, Virginia, 22920 (540)456-8667, (540)456-8002~Fax

Wines: Chardonnay, Gewürztraminer, Pinot Noir, Cabernet Sauvignon.

Tastings/tours available. Call for schedule. $3.00 fee per person for groups of 20 or more.

"Located in a beautiful setting with a winery utilizing gravity flow system and a cave for barrel aging."

Rebec Vineyards

2229 North Amherst Highway, Amherst, Virginia, 24521 (804)946-5168, (804)946-5168~Fax

Wines: Table Wines, Chardonnay, Riesling, Cabernet Sauvignon.

Tastings/tours available daily from 10am-5pm.

Gray Ghost Vineyards

14706 Lee Highway, Amissville, Virginia, 20106 (540)937-4869,(540)937-4869~Fax

Wines: Chardonnay, Cabernet Sauvignon, Cabernet Franc, Adieu (Late Harvest Vidal Blanc), Victorian White, Victorian Red, Vidal Blanc, Seyval Blanc.

Tastings/tours available Friday-Monday 11am-5pm.

"Internationally awarded wines. Immaculate vineyards and grounds. Southern hospitality at this family owned and operated winery."

Barboursville Vineyards

17655 Winery Road (P.O. Box 136), Barboursville, Virginia, 22923 (540)832-3824, (540)832-7572~Fax, www.barboursvillewine.com

Wines: European vinifers varietals.

Tastings daily, tours hourly on weekends. $3.00 fee. Classic Northern Italian restaurant on premises.

"Virginia's most-awarded winery since 1976. We are three destinations in one: hand-crafted wines, superb cuisine, and the ruins of Governor Barbour's mansion designed by Thomas Jefferson."

Burnley Vineyards and Winery

4500 Winery Lane, Barboursville, Virginia, 22923 (540)832-2828, (540)832-2280~Fax, www.b48.com/burnley

Wines: Table Wines, Fruit and Berry Wines, Chardonnay, Riesling, Cabernet Sauvignon.

Tastings/tours available April-December from 11am-5pm daily. January-March from 11am-5pm.

Totier Creek Vineyard and Winery

1652 Harris Creek Road, Charlottesville, Virginia, 22902   (804)979-7105, (804)293-2054~Fax

Wines: Table Wines, Chardonnay, Riesling, Merlot.

Tastings/tours available Wednesday-Sunday 11am-5pm.

Peaks of Otter Winery

Elmos Road, Bedford, Virginia, 24523   (540)586-3707, www.peaksofotterwinery.com

Wines: Table Wines, Fruit, Berry.

Tastings/tours available daily August through November from 8am-5pm. December-July by appointment.

Windy River Winery

20268 Terran Road, Beaverdam, Virginia, 23015   (804)449-6996, (804)449-6138~Fax, www.windyriverwinery.com

Wines: Chardonnay, Viognier, Cayuga, Wolf Blanc (Seyval), Ruby Blush, Rove, The Wolf (Cab. Franc), Cabernet Sauvignon, Merlot.

Tastings/tours available Thursday-Saturday from 12pm-5pm, and Sunday's from 1pm-5pm. $5.00 fee per person, includes glass.

"Windy River is Virginia's 50th Virginia winery. A small family business with great hospitality. Come visit and relax with fine wine."

First Colony Winery Ltd.

1650 Harris Creek Road, Charlottesville, Virginia, 22902, (804)979-7105, (804)293-2054~Fax

Wines: Chardonnay, Riesling, Merlot, Cabernet Sauvignon, Cabernet Franc.

Tastings/tours available from 10am-5pm daily. Gift shop on premises. Cheese and crackers available.

"Peaceful, secluded getaway for visitors offering a taste of friendly charm and fine wine, located in Virginia's Jefferson County."

Jefferson Vineyards

1353 Thomas Jefferson Parkway, Charlottesville, Virginia, 22902 (804)977-3042, (800)272-3042, (804)977-5459~Fax www.jeffersonvineyards.com

Wines: Chardonnay, Pinot Gris, Riesling, Cabernet Franc, Cabernet Sauvignon, Merlot, Meritage.

Tastings and tours daily from 11am-5pm.

"Thomas Jefferson convinced Italian Filippo Mazzei to establish a vineyard adjacent to Monticello. Today, on this same land, we produce nationally recognized wines."

Oakencroft Vineyard and Winery Corp.

1486 Oakencroft Lane, Charlottesville, Virginia, 22901   (804)296-4188, (804)293-6631~Fax, www.oakencroft.com

Wines: Countryside White, Chardonnay, Sweet Virginia, Merlot, Cabernet Sauvignon, Cabernet Franc, Countryside Red.

Tastings/Tours available April-December 7 days per week from 11am-5pm. Weekends only in March. Fee of $1.00 per person, or $3.00 per person and keep your wine glass.

"Lush green pastures, Blue Ridge Mountains, lake front, great place for picnic and afternoon enjoying the great taste of Virginia wines."

Tomahawk Mill Winery

9221 Anderson Mill Road, Chatham, Virginia, 24531   (804)432-1063, (804)432-2037~Fax, tomahawk@gamewood.net

Wines: Chardonnay, Cabernet Sauvignon, Pinot Noir, Mead, Apple, Concord, Tobacco Road Blues, and Vidal Blanc.

Tastings/tours Tuesday through Saturday 11am-5pm from March 15-December 15. $2.00 fee to be discounted from purchase for groups over 10.

"Enjoy fine wines in a water-powered grist mill built by a surviving confederate soldier after the Battle of Gettysburg."

Guide to Fine Wines

White Hall Vineyards

5190 Sugar Ridge Road, Crozet, Virginia, 22932   (804)823-8615, (804)823-4366~Fax, www.whitehallvineyards.com

Wines: Chardonnay, Pinot Gris, Merlot, Cabernet Franc, Reserve Chardonnay, Gewürztraminer, Cabernet Sauv. Soliterre.

Tastings/tours available Wednesday-Sunday from 11am-5pm. Closed December-February.

"Wines are consistent gold medal winners in the Virginia Governor's Cup competition. Our winery sits in the beautiful Blue Ridge."

Stonewall Vineyards and Winery

Route 2, Box 107A, Concord, Virginia, 24538   (804)993-2185, (804)993-3975~Fax

Wines: Table Wines, Mead, Cayuga, Chambourcin, Vidal.

Tastings/tours available daily from 11am-5pm.

Dominion Wine Cellars

One Winery Avenue, Culpeper, Virginia, 22701   (540)825-8772, (540)829-0377~Fax

Wines: Table Wines, Seyval, Vidal, Riesling.

Tastings/tours available Tuesday-Saturday 10am-5pm, Sunday's 11am-5pm. Closed Monday's.

Shenandoah Vineyards

3659 South Ox Road, Edinburg, Virginia, 22824   (540)984-8699, (540)984-9462~Fax, www.shentel.net/shenvine

Wines: Chardonnay, Chardonnay Founder's Reserve, Riesling, Shenandoah Blanc, Blusing Belle, Cabernet Sauvignon, Chambourcin, Shenandoah Ruby, Sweet Serenade, Fiesta, Raspberry Serenade.

Tastings/tours available, call for times. $5.00 fee per person for groups of 15 or more.

"Virginia's fourth oldest winery, oldest in Shenandoah Valley, established 1976. Beautiful Massanutten Mountain views, picnic tables, gift shop, tastings, tours."

Chateau Morrisette
287 Winery Road, Floyd, Virginia, 24091   (540)593-2865, (540)593-2868~Fax, www.chateaumorisette.com

Wines: Table Wines, Chardonnay.

Tastings/tours available Monday-Saturday 10am-5pm, Sunday 11am-5pm.

Villa Appalaccia Winery
Route 1, Box 661, Floyd, Virginia, 24091   (540)593-3100, www.villappalaccia.com

Wines: Table Wines, Cabernet Franc, Sangiovese, Pinot Grigio.

Tastings/tours available Saturday's and Sunday's 10am-5pm. Thursday, Friday

11-5, or by appointment.

Hartwood Winery, INC.
345 Hartwood Road, Fredericksburg, Virginia, 22406   (540)752-4893, (540)752-4893~Fax

Wines: Table Wines, Seyval Blanc, Vidal Blanc, Chambourcin.

Tastings/tours available Wednesday-Sunday 11am-6pm.

Horton Vineyards
6399 Spotswood Trail, Gordonsville, Virginia, 22942   (540)832-7440, (800)829-4633, (540)832-7187~Fax, http://www.hvwine.com

Wines: Varieties of Reds, Whites, Fruits, Desserts and After Dinner Wines, Sparkling Viognier.

Tastings/tours available 7 days per week from 10am-5pm. Closed Christmas, New Years and Thanksgiving.

"Taste the world of wine with our 30 plus wines including wines made from Rhone, Italian, Portuguese, and other noble varieties."

Guide to Fine Wines

Grayhaven

4675 East Grey Fox Circle, Gum Spring, Virginia, 23065   (804)556-3917, (804)556-3917~Fax.

Wines: Riesling, Vectal, Veyval, Foch, Red blends, White blends, most Dry.

Tastings/tours available Saturdays and Sunday from 9am-5pm, call to schedule other times.

"Tiny family vineyard and winery, picturesque setting with romantic atmosphere, sites for weddings, picnics, etc. Easy access from I-64."

Stonewall Vineyards and Winery

Route 2, Box 107A, Concord, Virginia, 24538   (804)993-2185, (804)993-3975~Fax

Wines: Table Wines, Mead, Cayuga, Chambourcin, Vidal.

Tastings/tours available daily from 11am-5pm.

The Rose Bower Vineyard and Winery

P. O. Box 126, State Route 686, Hampden-Sydney, Virginia, 23943 (804)223-8209, (804)223-3508~Fax

Wines: Table Wines, Dessert Wine, Rose Bower, Oak Chalet.

Landwirt Vineyard LLC

Route 2, box 286, Harrisonburg, Virginia, 22801 (540)833-6000, (540)833-6000~Fax

Wines: Table Wines, Riesling, Chardonnay, Cabernet Sauvignon.

Tastings/tours available Saturday's and Sunday's from 1pm-5pm.

Spotted Tavern Winery/Dodd Bros. Cidery

Route 612, Hartwood Road, Hartwood, Virginia, 22471   (540)752-4453,

Wines: Table Wine, Hard Cider, Fresh Cider, Seyval.

Tastings/tours available Saturday's and Sunday's from 12pm-4pm.

Shadwell-Windham

14727 Mountain Road, Hillsboro, Virginia, 20132   (540)668-6464,
(540)668-9652~Fax, www.shadwellwindhamwinery.com

Wines: Chardonnay, Riesling, Cab Franc, Merlot, Sauvignon Blanc, Cabernet Sauvignon, Vintner's Reserve.

Tastings/tours available from March-December on Saturday's from 12pm-6pm, and Sunday's from 2pm-6pm.

"Small farm winery near Short Hill Mountain. Family owned, many personal touches. New winery building sits near one acre pond."

Dye's Vineyard

RR 2, box 357, Honaker, Virginia, 24260   (540)873-4659, (540)873-4659~Fax

Wines: French Hybrid, Chardonnay, Cabernet Sauvignon.

Tastings/tours available Monday-Saturday from 1pm-dusk. Catered dinner available with wine on the third Saturday of the month at 7pm for $30.00 per couple.

"Only winery in SW Virginia area. Many years experience. Craft learned from German winemakers, rather than French. Unique."

Oasis Winery

14141 Hume Road, Hume, Virginia, 22639   (540)635-7627, (540)635-4653~Fax, www.oasiswine.com

Wines: Chardonnay, Cabernet Sauvignon, Merlot.

Tastings/tours available daily from 10am-5pm. Fee of $3.00 per person. Restaurant on premises.

"Rated top 10 in the world by the Wine Enthusiast Magazine!"

Misty Mountain Vineyard and Winery, INC.

HCR 02 Box 459, Madison, Virginia, 22727   (540)288-9908

Wines: Table Wines, Merlot, Cabernet Sauvignon, Chardonnay.

Tastings/tours available Monday-Sunday 11am-5pm.

Tarara

13648 Tarara Lane, Leesburg, Virginia, 20176   (703)771-7100, (703)771-8443~Fax, www.tarara.com

Wines: Pinot Gris, Chardonnay, Viognier, Cabernet Franc, Merlot, Cabernet Sauvignon, Chambourcin, Charval, Terra Rouge, Cameo, Wild River Red.

Tastings/tours available Wednesday through Monday from 11am-5pm. Weekends only in January and February. $3.00 fee per person, includes souvenir glass. Bed and Breakfast on site.

"Unique wine making cave, 475 acre farm. Located on the bluffs of the Potomac River, west of Washington D.C."

Prince Michel Vineyards and Rapipan River Vineyards

South Route 29, HCR 4, Box 77, Leon, Virginia, 22725   (540)347-3707, (540)547-3088~Fax, www.princemichel.com

Wines: Chardonnay, Merlot, Cabernet, Riesling, Gewürztraminer, Sweet Reserve, Sparkling Virginia Brut.

Free self-guided tours of museum and production facility available. Tastings $2.00. Call for times. Restaurant on premises.

"Prince Michel Vineyards, Virginia's leading estate winery, features over a hundred planted acres, wine museum, French restaurant and luxurious suites."

Linden Vineyards

3708 Harrels Corner Road, Linden Virginia, 22642   (540)364-1997, (540)364-3894~Fax, www.lindenvineyards.com

Wines: Red Bordeaux variety blends, Chardonnay, Sauvignon Blanc.

Tastings/tours available Wednesday through Sunday from April-November, 11am-5pm. Saturday's and Sunday's from December-March from 11am-5pm.

"Passionate wines and wine growers-all with great character, personality and verve."

Mountain Cove Vineyards and Wine Garden

1362 Fortunes Cove Lane, Lovingston, Virginia, 22949   (804)263-5392, (804)263-8590~Fax

Wines: Tinto (Cabernet Sauvignon), Chardonnay, Skyline White, Blackberry, Peach, Apple, Ginseng Gold.

Tastings/tours available Wednesday through Sunday from 12pm-6pm.

"Located in scenic valley, a quiet place for a picnic or walk on country roads. Our tours do truly inform."

Guilford Ridge Vineyard

328 Running Pine Road, Luray, Virginia, 22835   (540)778-3853

Wines: Table Wines.

Tastings/ tours available by appointment.

Naked Mountain Vineyard and Winery

2947 Leeds Manor Road, Markham, Virginia, 22643, (540)364-1609, (540)364-4870~Fax, www.nakedmtn.com

Wines: Chardonnay, Riesling, Sauv Blanc, Cab Sauv, Cab Franc.

Tastings/tours available Wednesday-Sunday in March-December from 11am-5pm. $3.00 fee per person.

"Naked Mountain is a Virginia winery that serious wine circles consistently note for excellence. Views from deck are breath taking."

Swedenburg Estate Vineyard, Valley View Farm

23595 Winery Lane, Middleburg, Virginia, 20117   (540)687-5219

Wines: Chardonnay, Riesling, Cabernet Sauvignon, Pinot Noir, Seyval.

Tastings available daily from 10am-4pm for a $1.00 fee. No tours except for groups of ten or more with advance notice. Fee of $3.00 per person for tour.

"European style wines, French oriented. As in similar France soil, no fertilizer or irrigation used, all left to Mother Nature!"

Guide to Fine Wines

Piedmont Vineyards and Winery
P. O. Box 286, Middleburg, Virginia, 22117   (540)687-5528, (540)687-5777~Fax

Wines: Table Wines.

Tastings/tours available daily from 10am-5pm.

Wintergreen Winery
462 Winery Lane, Nellysford, Virginia, 22958   (804)361-2519,(804)361-1510~Fax, www.wintergreenwinery.com

Wines: Chardonnay, Riesling, Merlot, Cabernet Franc, Cabernet Sauvignon, Apple, Raspberry Dessert.

Tastings/tours available daily in April-October from 10am-6pm, November-March, 10am-5pm.

"Experience award-winning wines, renowned hospitality, and panoramic views at this family owned winery nestled against the Blue Ridge Mountains."

Ingleside Plantation Vineyards
5872 Leedstown Road, Oak Grove, Virginia, 22443   (804)224-8687, (804)224-8573~Fax, www.ipwine.com

Wines: Chardonnay, Merlot, Cabernet Sauvignon, Ciognier, Pinot Gris, Brut Champagne.

Tastings/tours available Monday-Saturday from 10am-5pm, Sunday's 12pm-5pm.

$2.00 fee per person for groups over ten. Cheese, crackers, sausage available.

"Oldest/largest Virginia winery. Family owned since 1890. Built as Washington Academy in 1834, near birth place of Robert E. Lee."

Sharp Rock Vineyards
5 Sharp Rock Road, Sperryville, Virginia, 22740   (540)987-9700,(540)987-9031~Fax, www.sharprock.com

Wines: Table Wines, Chardonnay, Sauvignon Blanc, Cabernet Franc.

Tastings/tours available Saturday and Sunday from12pm-5pm.

Beaux Vineyards

36888 Breaux Vineyards Lane, Purcellville, Virginia, 20132   (800)492-9961,
(540)668-6283~Fax, www.breauxvineyards.com

Wines: Sauvignon Blanc, Viognier, Chardonnay, ("Barrel Fermented" and
"Madeleine's"), Seyval Blanc, Vidal Blanc, "Lafayette" Cabernet Franc, Merlot, Cabernet
Sauvignon, "Breaux Soleil" Lake Harvest Vidal Blanc.

Tastings/tours available daily from May to October 11am-6pm, November-April 11am-
5pm. $3.00 fee for groups of 8 or more. Upscale picnic fare available, bread, cheeses,
pate', etc.. Decorative items and gifts for sale.

"Beautiful setting at the foot of the Blue Ridge and Short Hill Mountains. Patio
Madeleine outdoor seating surrounded by vineyards."

Rockbridge Vineyard, INC.

State Route 606, Raphine, Virginia   (540)377-6204, (888)511-WINE

Wines: Table Wines, Fruit, Berry, Vidal Blanc, Chardonnay, Cabernet Sauvignon.

Tastings/tours available May-December Wednesday-Sunday from 12pm-5pm. During
the month of April, open Saturday and Sunday 12pm-5pm.

Valhalla Vineyards

6500 Mount Chestnut Road, Roanoke, Virginia, 24018 (540)925-9463,
(540)772-7858~Fax, www.valhallawines.com

Wines: Table Wines, Chardonnay, Sangiovese, Cabernet Sauvignon.

Tastings/tours available. Call for hours.

Rose River Vineyards

Route 648, Syria, Virginia, 22743 (540)923-4050

Wines: Table Wines, Fruit, Berry, Cabernet Sauvignon, Chardonnay.

Tastings/tours available April-December on Saturday's and Sunday's from 10am-5pm.
By appointment only January-March.

Lake Anna Winery

5621 Courthouse Road, Spotsylvania, Virginia, 22553, (540)895-5085,
(540)895-9749~Fax, www.lawinery.com

Wines: Chardonnay, Seyval Blanc, Merlot, Cabernet Sauvignon, Semi-Dry Red, White,
and Blush.

Tastings/tours available Wednesday-Saturday from 11am-5pm, Sunday's from 1pm-
5pm. Closed December 24-January 31. $2.00 fee to taste more than four wines.

"Beautiful tasting room with view of the vineyards. Shaded picnic area. Great place to
relax and enjoy the Virginia countryside."

Loudon Valley Vineyards

38516 Charlestown Pike, Waterford, Virginia, 20197 (540)882-3375,
www.loudonvalleyvineyards.com

Wines: Chardonnay, Riesling, Vinifera White, Rose, Merlot, Cabernet Sauvignon,
Cabernet Franc, Pinot Noir, Sangiovese, Nebbiolo, Suavignon Blanc.

Tastings/tours available April through December, Friday-Sunday from 11am-5pm.
January-March, Saturday-Sunday from 11am-5pm. Call ahead for groups over eight
people.

"Spectacular setting. View of Blue Ridge and Catoctin Mountains from decks, winter
fires. Friendly/knowledgeable staff and award winning wines."

The Williamsburg Winery, Ltd.

5800 Wessex Hundred, Williamsburg, Virginia, 23185 (757)229-0999,
(757)229-0911~Fax, www.williamsburgwineryltd.com

Wines: Varieties of Red, Dessert, White Johannisberg Riesling, Lord Culpeper
Reserve, and Filippo Mazzei Reserve.

Tastings/tours available daily from Monday-Saturday 10am-5:30pm, Sunday from
12pm-5:30pm. $6.00 fee per person. Restaurant on premises.

"The Williamsburg Winery is dedicated to blending age-old winemaking concepts with
the advantages of modern technology."

Willowcroft Farm Vineyards

38906 Mount Gilead Road, Leesburg, Virginia, 20175   (703)777-8161, (703)777-8157~Fax, www.willowcroftwine.com

Wines: Table Wine, Fruit, Berry, Chardonnay, Cabernet Sauvignon, Cabernet Franc.

Tastings/tours available Wed-Sunday 11am-5pm, January by appointment. February open weekends only.

Autumn Hill Vineyards

301 River Drive, Stanardsville, Virginia, 22973 (804)985-6100, www.autumnhillwine.com

Wines: Cabernet Sauvignon, Merlot, Cabernet Franc, Chardonnay.

Tastings/tours available on certain weekends only, call for dates. Fee involved.

"Autumn Hill vineyards and it's Blue Ridge Winery grows 13 acres of European Vines."

Deer Meadow Vineyard

199 Vintage Lane, Winchester, Virginia, 22602   (800)653-6632, (561)423-0420~Fax

Wines: Chardonnay, Cabernet Sauvignon, Marechat Foch, Chambourcin, Golden Blush, Afternoon of the Fawn.

Tastings/tours available Wednesday through Sunday from March-December from 11am-5pm.

WEST VIRGINIA

Little Hungary Farm Winery

Route 6, Box 323, Buckhannon, West Virginia, 26201   (304)472-6634

Wines: Mead.

Tastings/tours available anytime.

Guide to Fine Wines

Daniel Vineyards

200 Twin Oaks Road, Glen View, West Virginia, 25827   (304)252-9750, (304)252-6011~Fax, www.danielvineyards.com

Wines: Table Wine, Fruit, Berry, Seyval, Vidal, Cayuga.

Tastings/tours available Monday-Saturday 10am-6pm, Sunday's 1pm-6pm.

A.T. Gift Company

Route 3, Box 802, Harpers Ferry, West Virginia, 25425   (304)876-6680, (304)876-2757~Fax

Wines: Sweet Fruit and Berry Wines.

Tastings/tours by appointment.

"Our winery has produced the only West Virginia wine served at the White House and on Capital Hill in Washington, D.C."

Fisher Ridge Wine Co.

Rt 1, Box 108 A Fisher Ridge Road, Liberty, West Virginia, 25124 (304)342-8702, (304)352-8702~Fax, www.fisherridgewine.com

Wines: Chardonnay/Blanc de Blanc, Cellarmaster Reserve Red and White, Maidens Kiss, Barrel Selection 1998/Blush.

Tastings/tours available by appointment.

"Oldest existing West Virginia winery, est. 1979. Only winery located within the Kanawha River Valley Viticultural District."

Schneider's Winery

North of U.S. 50 on Jersey Mountain Road, Romney, West Virginia, 26757 (304)822-7434, (304)822-5944~Fax

Wines: Table Wine, Fruit, Berry, Vidal, Concord, Marechal Foch.

Tastings/tours available Wednesday-Saturday 12pm-6pm, Sunday's 1pm-6pm.

Forks of Cheat Winery

2811 Stewartstown Road, Morgantown, West Virginia, 26508 (304)598-2019, (304)598-2019~Fax, www.wvwines.com

Wines: Villard Blanc, Seyval Blanc, Vidal Blanc, Schwarze Bar, Niagara, Vin Gris, Merlot, Cabernet Sauvignon, Burgundy, Baco Noir, Foch, Leon Millot, Chambourcin, DeChaunac, Van Buren, Blackberry, Strawberry, Raspberry, Blueberry, Pear, Apple, Plum, Spiced Apple, Spice, Port.

Tastings/tours available. Call for hours.

"West Virginia's largest winery, producing extensive variety of wines in a unique atmosphere amidst the breathtaking mountain vistas."

Potomac Highland Winery

Rural Route 6, Box 6980, Keyser, West Virginia, 26726 (304)788-3066, www.winesacrossamerica.com

Wines: Chardonnay, Riesling, Seyval Blanc, Aurore Pinot Noir, Chambourcin, Chancellor, Meritage, Seyval Blush.

Tastings/tours available. Please call ahead.

"We grow Vinifera grapes in West Virginia resulting in special wines, Chardonnay, Riesling, Pinot Noir, and Meritage."

Robert F. Pliska and Company Winery

101 Piterra Place, Purgitsville, West Virginia, 26852 (304)289-3493, (304)289-3900~Fax, www.pliskawinery@raven-villages.net

Wines: Ridge Runner Gold, Red, and Semi-Dry, Mountain Mama, Mountain Betty, Mountain Elsie (Semi Sweet Fruit Wines), Dry varietals.

Tastings/tours by appointment.

"Considered one of top 100 wineries to visit. Julia Child, N.C. Chefs Association, U.S. Embassy in Paris featured our wines. "

Guide to Fine Wines

Kirkwood Winery

1350 Phillips Run Road, Summersville, West Virginia, 26651 (304)872-7332,
www.kirkwood-wine.com

Wines: Vegetable, Red, Blush, Fruit.

Tastings/tours available daily. Call for times.

"Home of the Grape Stomping Festival. Visit our country store and delight your palate
with West Virginia's finest wine."

Lambert's Vintage Wines, LLC.

Route 1, Box 332-1, Weston, West Virginia, 26452   (304)269-3973, (304)269-4903,
(304)472-8486~Fax

Wines: Table Wine, Fruit, Berry, Merlot, Chardonnay.

Tastings/tours available Monday-Saturday 11am-7pm, Sunday's 1pm-5pm.

About the Author
VICTOR L. ROBILIO, JR.

President of the Victor L. Robilio Co., Inc. "Worldwide Importer and Wholesaler of Wines, Food and Spirits"

Travels to: Hungary, France, Spain, California, Washington, Germany and Italy for wine buying trips

Member of the Chevalier Du Tastevin (Burgundy Wine Brotherhood)

Master Commander, Tennessee Chapter of the "Brotherhood of the Knights of the Vine," founder of the Tennessee Chapter in 1979. Provost General of the Southeastern United States

Graduate of Sommelier Society of America, California, French and Italian Wine Study Courses

Author of the book, *The Redneck Guide to Wine Snobbery*, which is in its third printing and was newly revised in 1998

Lecturer and author of wine articles, formally "Wind and Spirits." Writer for "Memphis Home and Garden" magazine and host of a TV cable Channel 18, "Memphis Makers."

Premium gift books from PREMIUM PRESS AMERICA include:

I'LL BE DOGGONE

CATS OUT OF THE BAG

GREAT AMERICAN CIVIL WAR

GREAT AMERICAN GOLF

GREAT AMERICAN OUTDOORS

GREAT AMERICAN GUIDE TO FINE
WINES

ANGELS EVERYWHERE

MIRACLES

SNOW ANGELS

ABSOLUTELY ALABAMA

AMAZING ARKANSAS

FABULOUS FLORIDA

GORGEOUS GEORGIA

SENSATIONAL SOUTH CAROLINA

TERRIFIC TENNESSEE

TREMENDOUS TEXAS

VINTAGE VIRGINIA

TITANIC TRIVIA

BILL DANCE'S FISHING TIPS

DREAM CATCHERS

AMERICA THE BEAUTIFUL

PREMIUM PRESS AMERICA routinely updates existing titles and frequently adds new topics to its growing line of premium gift books. Books are distributed though gift and specialty shops, and bookstores nationwide. If, for any reason, books are not available in your area, please contact the local distributor listed above or contact the Publisher direct by calling 1-800-891-7323. To see our complete backlist and current books, you can visit our website at www.premiumpressamerica.com. Thank you.

Great Reading. Premium Gifts.